# The Essentials of Science, Grades 7–12

# PRIORITIES *in* PRACTICE

# The Essentials of Science, Grades 7–12

## Effective Curriculum, Instruction, and Assessment

Rick Allen

Association for Supervision and Curriculum Development • Alexandria, Virginia USA

Association for Supervision and Curriculum Development
1703 N. Beauregard St. • Alexandria, VA 22311-1714 USA
Phone: 800-933-2723 or 703-578-9600 • Fax: 703-575-5400
Web site: www.ascd.org • E-mail: member@ascd.org
Author guidelines: www.ascd.org/write

*About the Author:* Rick Allen is a writer and project manager at ASCD. He has worked as a writer and editor in education journalism for 12 years.

Gene R. Carter, *Executive Director;* Nancy Modrak, *Publisher;* Julie Houtz, *Director of Book Editing & Production;* Miriam Goldstein, *Project Manager;* Georgia Park, *Senior Graphic Designer;* Keith Demmons, *Typesetter;* Sarah Plumb, *Production Specialist*

All Web links in this book are correct as of the publication date below but may have become inactive or otherwise modified since that time. If you notice a deactivated or changed link, please e-mail books@ascd. org with the words "Link Update" in the subject line. In your message, please specify the Web link, the book title, and the page number on which the link appears.

PAPERBACK ISBN-13: 978-1-4166-0572-0          ASCD product #107119 s11/07
Also available as an e-book through ebrary, netLibrary, and many online booksellers (see Books in Print for the ISBNs).

Quantity discounts for the paperback edition only: 10–49 copies, 10%; 50+ copies, 15%; for 1,000 or more copies, call 800-933-2723, ext. 5634, or 703-575-5634. For desk copies: member@ascd.org.

**Library of Congress Cataloging-in-Publication Data**

Allen, Rick, 1959-
  The essentials of science, grades 7-12 : effective curriculum, instruction, and assessment / Rick Allen.
    p. cm. -- (Priorities in practice)
  Includes bibliographical references and index.
  ISBN 978-1-4166-0572-0 (pbk. : alk. paper)  1.  Science—Study and teaching (Secondary) 2.  Science—Study and teaching (Middle school)  I. Title.

  Q181.A414 2007
  507.1'2—dc22

                              2007027255

16 15 14 13 12 11 10 09 08 07     1 2 3 4 5 6 7 8 9 10 11 12

# PRIORITIES *in* PRACTICE

## The Essentials of Science, Grades 7–12

# Preface

When I was a novice newspaper reporter, my editors inevitably accompanied story assignments with this solid piece of advice: "Go back to the library and check the clips." So instead of obeying my first hasty impulse to start placing calls to sources or to head out to get the scoop, I would calmly start by poring through a fat bundle of newspaper clips pulled from the newsroom library's shelves. This "old news" gave me the background on the topic, the people, or the events that others had written about before me. Reading those clips gave me a sense of the cyclical nature of the news. There was plenty of evidence to see that the past does tend to repeat itself, George Santayana's oft-quoted admonition notwithstanding.

That's why, when I began to write *Priorities in Practice: The Essentials of Science, Grades 7–12,* I decided to check out the archives of ASCD's magazine *Educational Leadership.* Known familiarly in the ASCD office as *EL,* the magazine has chronicled the ups and downs and all arounds of K–12 education for more than 60 years—since 1943, to be exact.

In *EL's* electronic archives (www.ascd.org), I found a number of interesting articles that highlighted calls for reforms in science education that sound awfully familiar today. Issues have ranged from concern over a lack of K–12 articulation in science curricula to a call for curriculum reform to promote a deeper understanding of science concepts and processes (Barnard, 1962) to the perennial fear that rival countries surpass the United States in science instruction (National Science Foundation, 1981).

Then I read George DeBoer's excellent book, *A History of Ideas in Science Education: Implications for Practice* (1991), which provided a perspective of science education reform over the last 200 years within the larger context of changes in society's understanding of education and learning. Like many an evolution, reform occurs slowly, with occasional fits and starts.

So where is secondary-level science heading today?

After visiting schools and talking to a variety of researchers, teachers, and administrators, I can report that secondary science education is at a curious crossroads as a result of the current standards movement. The renewed focus on scientific inquiry—which, prior to the last decade, had its widest currency in the post-*Sputnik* reforms of the late 1950s and the 1960s (Kelly & Ponder, 1997)—has combined with new research on how people learn, so that the ideal science classrooms have become student-centered places of learning and, as such, are moving more slowly. The implied decree of standards-based education to "teach less better" (as opposed to teaching more less) might be finally getting a proper hearing in high schools, as school leaders figure out how to hone the science curriculum to focus on major concepts.

The best science teachers also recognize the balance that science classes need to achieve between teaching mastery of content and understanding the nature of science as science. Students appreciate the unique role that science can play in the school curriculum when they understand the practices of scientific inquiry, from raising and answering their own questions about the natural world to engaging in the semistructured or "guided" labs common to middle and high schools. It seems that the more initiative allowed students in the lab or with other inquiry activities, the greater their engagement with science content. Such engagement provides the groundwork for at least the possibility that students could one day become scientists.

During the course of my research, I also learned that science education grapples with the societal needs of each generation. Some reform ideas will seem familiar because many of modern society's needs have not changed greatly over time. Yet some calls for reform are unique to an age. I'm pleased to include Chapter 3, which profiles research on model science curricula, and Chapter 4, which covers research on urban science education, because both offer holistic strategies to address the complex problems of the achievement gap, equity, and resources in the science classroom.

In addition, *The Essentials of Science, Grades 7–12* provides a concise overview of major trends in secondary science education (Chapter 1); insight into the importance of backward curriculum design (Chapter 2); lively examples of classroom practice from award-winning teachers (Chapter 3); strategies for dealing with both day-to-day and NCLB assessments (Chapter 5); and examples of effective professional development (Chapter 6).

This book was made possible by the generosity of many science educators who offered me a window into their classroom practice or research. In particular, I would like to thank Alan Colburn, Paula Young, Michael Fryda, Dat Le, and Jaimie Foster, as well as the urban science education researchers Kenneth Tobin, Okhee Lee, Gale Seiler, and Christopher Emdin, whose work reminds us all of the importance of keeping intact the integrity of the whole student within the school setting. Finally, I would like to especially thank my wife, Joana, for her unstinting support throughout.

# Trends in Secondary Science Education

*To give good instruction in the sciences requires of the teacher more work than to give good instruction in mathematics or the languages—the sooner this fact is recognized by those who have the management of schools, the better for all concerned.*

—*Report of the Committee on Secondary School Studies*
(the "Committee of Ten"), 1893

Imagine if in some Dickensian manner, Charles Eliot—chair of the Committee of Ten, former president of Harvard University, and primary shaper of the U.S. high school curriculum for the 20th century—could be whisked from a ghostly campus at Harvard Yard and installed in a typical high school science class today. Once Eliot had a chance to look around, what would he see? Would secondary science as he and the Committee of Ten had envisioned it in their influential recommendations have changed very much? Would he be able to give the science teacher a coffee break, perhaps, and pick up the class as coteacher?

Yes and no.

Much has changed in the realm of high school science since Eliot's days. Today, students are expected to master a far greater scope and depth of scientific knowledge. In biology, students might be separating DNA from onion or bean cells or debating the morality of genetic testing and cloning. In physics, students might be trying to understand nano-technology, which uses molecular theory to make tiny devices, such as gears, wires, and tubes, billionths of a meter in length. In earth and space science—which Eliot would have viewed as two separate disciplines, geology and astronomy—students would be learning the basics of the rock cycle, as they had for decades, but they might also be discussing the latest theory about the moon's formation from the residue of an almighty crash of two protoplanets during the universe's earliest period of existence.

What else about this 21st century school might surprise Eliot? The number of students enrolled, for starters, along with the variety of races, ethnicities, cultures, and languages represented in the student body. If Eliot left the science class to find a newspaper in the faculty lounge, he might read an article about the great expectations that society and schools have for students in the sciences. During an age that has largely given itself over to the ascendancy of science and technology, governments and businesses worldwide are counting on the scientific intellectual might of their respective nations' rising generations to ensure a strong position in the global economy. As science curriculum expert Rodger Bybee observes, "Now competitors are emerging in fast-growing economies like Singapore, China, and South Korea. And there are more competitors. The goal [of the United States] is economic competitiveness, which is much more abstract than the goal of going to the moon and back." This last goal, along with fears of Soviet technological domination, was what fueled U.S. science reform in the post-*Sputnik* era.

Still, aside from these changes, many features of U.S. science classes have stayed the same during the last century or so: lectures, textbooks, demonstrations and labs, and the 10th–12th grade sequence of biology, chemistry, and physics. In addition, high school science students still study human discovery and invention and the timeless understandings about the natural world. Eliot might just find enough familiar today to believe that the Committee of Ten had indeed arranged a science curriculum for the ages. But not everyone sees it that way.

"We're teaching 1800s content in a 21st century world on an agrarian 1900s schedule," says Steven Long, high school division director for the National Science Teachers Association (NSTA). Teaching methods have changed very little for the majority of science teachers in the United States: "We still lecture; we still write on the board; we still have textbooks and expect students to take part in rote memorization," Long notes. "There's too little use of inquiry and project-based learning. That's in my own classroom—I'm not just pointing fingers at others. Why is it so? It's the way we were taught, it's comfortable, and it's what parents expect. It's the way our schools are set up to function."

But that could all be changing. With the increasing dissemination of the National Research Council (NRC)'s *National Science Education Standards*, published in 1996, public pressure to educate students for scientific literacy and a deeper conceptual understanding of science has been steadily increasing. In the ongoing race for education reform, secondary science has continually been outmuscled in a crowded field: first by reading and math, and then, within its own ranks, by elementary science. But this time around, secondary science teaching could really change, due to the convergence of government and business support, wider dissemination of new research on how students learn, and increasing calls for a major overhaul of high school education.

## Awaiting an NCLB Effect

New No Child Left Behind (NCLB) regulations that mandate science testing have given the secondary science education field another reason to reassess its practice. Starting with the 2007–2008 school year, annual science testing is to take place for one grade in each of three grade ranges: 3–5, 6–9, and 10–12. Although state science testing will not count in the measure of adequate yearly progress (AYP) that determines a school's failure or success, some science educators consider the "official" attention on science a positive move that casts the spotlight beyond the twin concerns of reading and math. Others believe that because science does not figure into AYP, it will hardly make a blip on the NCLB radar screen.

Nonetheless, NCLB testing can give education leaders a more complete picture of student progress in science. Many expect these tests to initially confirm the mediocre performance shown by previous large-scale assessments, such as the National Assessment of Educational Progress (NAEP). Science education experts give secondary science teaching in the United States a low-*C* average, and some think even that is too generous. Highly motivated, usually white suburban students in affluent, resource-rich high schools are learning science just fine, experts say; it's the rest who are falling short. *The Nation's Report Card: Science 2005* showed that only 18 percent of 12th graders could be rated as "proficient" in science, whereas 54 percent of students were rated "basic" (Grigg, Lauko, & Brockway, 2006). Numerous reports confirm the decline in U.S. science education, including the Trends in International Mathematics and Science Study (TIMSS), which measures science achievement in countries across the globe, and *The Nation's Report Card: Science 2005 Trial Urban District Assessment*, which addresses the failure of urban science education. No matter how science education is sliced and diced, it is found wanting.

Although NCLB testing may at first merely confirm this fact, science education researchers hope that the need for regular science testing will prompt new approaches to science assessment: "One of the things we have to be concerned about is testing for what we really value in science education. We're really looking for conceptual understanding rather than testing students on factoids and concrete information," says Linda Froschauer, president of NSTA.

Nevertheless, testing for conceptual understanding—not to mention science skills and the processes of scientific inquiry—will require the development of innovative approaches that could be years away, according to assessment experts. Iris Weiss, a science education researcher at Horizon Research in Chapel Hill, North Carolina, notes that "right now, whether it's the college level, the high school level, or any other level of science education, one of our biggest problems is we don't know how to measure very well the things we care about. As a result, we measure things we know how to measure, which tend to be vocabulary."

Weiss illustrates how hard it is to get beyond the mind-set of testing for discrete facts: "Years ago, one of the states had a performance assessment with this incredible setup that had kids rolling cars down ramps and all that. But the questions they had were along the lines of, 'This is called _____ energy.'" Despite the elaborate equipment, the chance to really probe student understanding about potential and kinetic energy was lost, the content glossed over with a few vocabulary questions.

Weiss concedes that measuring conceptual understanding is "exceptionally difficult." It takes "10 attempts to get 1 good test item," she says. Her research group, currently involved in a test-writing project, interviews students taking pilot tests to determine that when students answer an item correctly, they "get it right for the right reason"—and that when they get the answer wrong, they "get it wrong for the right reason," Weiss adds. In other words, the test item has to reveal which elements or notions within a concept are clear to the student, and which ones are not.

"Just like money drives a business, and [the business owners] know whether they are making a profit so that they can decide whether they need to retool their processes, assessments are the bottom line for education," Weiss suggests. "If we don't measure what we need to be measuring—what we think we're measuring and what we want to measure—then we're driving it all in the wrong direction."

## Making Science Meaningful

*National Science Education Standards*, in circulation for more than 10 years, defines the content goals for good K–12 science programs, including physics, chemistry, biology, and earth and space science. The standards also address, among other topics, important concepts about the nature of science; the relation of science to society; the development of science throughout history; and best practices of science teaching, professional development, and district programs.

Robert Yager, a science education reformer for nearly half a century, has long maintained that teaching science in connection to social issues equips students for a life of scientific and technological literacy in a modern society. Decades since he first promoted the Science-Technology-Society (STS) approach, Yager still considers it a healthy antidote to "book science." STS aims to integrate the various disciplines of secondary science in way that is relevant to students' lives and to the real world. He wants current science reforms to focus on "the four less familiar content facets" found in the national science education standards (Yager, 2005):

1. Science for society and personal challenges.
2. Technology.

3. History and philosophy of science.

4. Science as inquiry.

To point out the benefits of helping students to make meaning-ful connections between science and their own lives and society, Yager recounts the experience of a high school chemistry teacher who offered to teach science to vocational education students so that he could avoid filling a dreaded 9th grade algebra slot. The science students, mostly girls training to be hairstylists, were planning to enter the workforce right out of high school. The school allowed the teacher flexibility to fashion a science curriculum related to his students' planned careers, and the students told him that they wanted to focus on studying ozone because they would be wielding a lot of hair spray on the job. So the students learned about the chemistry of ozone and its effect on the envi-ronment, and they visited 3rd grade classes to teach younger students what they had learned. To raise awareness of the importance of ozone to a stable ecology, they organized an Ozone Depletion Day at the school, even engaging the support of the city's mayor.

By the end of the course, the hairdressing students had learned about pH and acids, solutions and compounds, and just about "everything in the chemistry book—including the periodic table of elements," Yager says. The irony, he adds with a chuckle, is that the college prep students started complaining that they were stuck doing cookbook labs while the hairdressing students were having all the fun. Yager concludes that these students were able to master the chemistry because they discovered the relevance that the science concepts had in their own lives.

Yager believes that teachers, students, and schools should play an integral role in developing curriculum. Yet schools often adopt whole-sale a science curriculum that has been developed in a kind of realm of ideal science, he suggests. Even popular kit-based curricula, a reaction to the excesses of rote science learning, "can be very poorly used," he says: "Some kit curricula are innovative, but when there's a teacher's manual, the teachers know the answer, and they revert to the same old thing: 'I know the answer, and here's what it is.' There's no inquiry. There's no thinking. It becomes another cookbook lesson, even though the lessons raise interesting ideas to follow."

## Understanding Scientific Inquiry

Science education reformers have long urged the use of a flexible model of scientific inquiry that moves beyond the static and seemingly closed-ended model of the "scientific method." Like the five-paragraph essay model taught in English classes, the scientific method as typically presented in science classes may be serviceable but is ultimately limited in scope. The authors of *National Science Education Standards*—which calls for primary and secondary students to be able to understand and carry out scientific inquiry—agree. In fact, they state that their call for inquiry "should not be interpreted as advocating a 'scientific method'" (NRC, 1996, p. 144). Although effective inquiry has a certain logical progression, the authors maintain, it is not rigid, and it involves engaging in multifaceted activities. The NRC's standards provide a list of the abilities that secondary students need to effectively conduct inquiry in the classroom. Middle school students should be able to

- Identify questions that can be answered through scientific investigations.
- Design and conduct a scientific investigation.
- Use appropriate tools and techniques to gather, analyze, and interpret data.
- Develop descriptions, explanations, predictions, and models using evidence.
- Think critically and logically to make the relationships between evidence and explanations.
- Recognize and analyze alternative explanations and predictions.
- Communicate scientific procedures and explanations.
- Use mathematics in all aspects of scientific inquiry. (NRC, 1996, pp. 145, 148)

High school students should be able to

- Identify questions and concepts that guide scientific investigations.
- Design and conduct scientific investigations.

• Use technology and mathematics to improve investigations and communications.

• Formulate and revise scientific explanations and models using logic and evidence.

• Recognize and analyze alternative explanations and models.

• Communicate and defend a scientific argument. (NRC, 1996, pp. 175, 176)

Many other experts also support the practice of inquiry in the secondary science classroom. The book *Doing Good Science in Middle School: A Practical Guide to Inquiry-Based Instruction* (Jorgenson, Cleveland, & Vanosdall, 2004) notes that the use of inquiry keeps young adolescents interested in science. During a time of considerable physical and cognitive development, an overreliance on textbooks, direct instruction, seatwork, and lectures can tax students' emerging abilities to sit still, concentrate, and deal with higher-level abstract knowledge. The authors assert that "teachers in the middle grades are charged with lighting the fires of 'finding out,' cultivating the innate adolescent passion for discovery, rather than snuffing it out with too much lecture or too many worksheets" (Jorgenson et al., 2004).

Despite inquiry's crucial role in science education and the clear measurements laid out by the NRC's standards, however, the definition of inquiry and the reality of inquiry practices vary greatly among science teachers, scientists, and researchers. University of South Carolina science education professor Stephen Thompson studied scientists and middle school teachers who worked together to implement scientific inquiry in the classroom as part of a reform effort to advance classroom understanding about the nature of science. On the basis of his observations and interviews with teachers, Thompson developed a framework to help teachers pinpoint their own inquiry-based practices on a continuum ranging from *technical inquiry* (which views scientific knowledge as fixed and absolute) to *substantive inquiry* (which views some scientific knowledge as tentative and values human creativity and new approaches for understanding phenomena or data), as well as ascertain the extent (from *low* to *high*) of teachers' application of those different levels of inquiry (see Figure 1.1).

| FIGURE 1.1 | | | |
|---|---|---|---|
| The Inquiry Framework | | | |
| | Technical | | Substantive | |
| | Low | High | Low | High |
| **Scientific Knowledge** | Fixed and absolute. | *Less* fixed and absolute. | Subject to change as new knowledge is acquired. | *Fixed* when it provides utility, and *tentative* when its lack of utility has been exposed. |
| **Scientific Method** | Linear, step-wise method used in the verification or creation of knowledge. | Series of steps used to investigate scientific questions in any order needed. | Multiple methods of investigation without understanding of factors that determine method choice. | Multiple methods of investigation with understanding of factors that determine method choice. |
| **Creativity in Inquiry** | Knowledge created during scientific inquiry is objective, not the product of human imagination, inference, or creativity. | Human imagination, inference, and creativity are aspects of some parts of scientific inquiry. | Human imagination, inference, and creativity are used in all aspects of scientific inquiry. | New ideas are examined through means that don't follow prescribed methods. Knowledge can be created in the mind and then verified "after the fact." |
| **Empirical Basis** | Relationship among questions, methods, data, and interpretations not clear. | Relationship among questions, methods, data, and interpretations learned out of context. | Relationship among questions, methods, data, and interpretations learned within context of genuine problem-solving activities but not explicitly addressed. | Relationship among questions, methods, data, and interpretations learned within context of genuine problem-solving activities and explicitly addressed. |
| **Subjective Nature** | All scientists reach similar conclusions from the same investigation. | Scientists can reach different conclusions from the same investigation. | Scientists can reach different conclusions from the same investigation based on prior experiences and "ways of knowing." Factors that influence conclusions not clear. | Scientists can reach different conclusions from the same investigation based on prior experiences and "ways of knowing." Explicit attention is drawn to factors that influence conclusions. |

The inquiry framework defines different aspects of scientific inquiry across a spectrum that, theoretically, could include every venue from science classrooms to science research labs. "The framework brings to light the fact that science is more than the body of knowledge within the fields of biology, chemistry, and physics," and it can be a means for teachers to see where their beliefs and practices fit on the spectrum of scientific inquiry, Thompson says.

The framework takes into account teachers' understanding of the following factors:

- The tentative nature of scientific knowledge.
- The existence and steps of the scientific method.
- The role of creativity in science.
- The empirical basis of scientific inquiry.
- The subjective nature of knowledge creation in science.

Thompson wanted to help teachers shed light on their own understanding of inquiry without calling their positions along the spectrum "right" or "wrong." For example, a teacher operating at the low end of technical inquiry would see the scientific method as a "linear, step-wise method" used to create knowledge, whereas a teacher operating at the high end of technical inquiry might freely reorder the steps to investigate a scientific question. Similarly, a teacher functioning at the low end of substantive inquiry might use multiple methods of investigation without necessarily understanding the factors behind those choices, whereas a teacher functioning at the high end would know the reasons behind her choices (Thompson, 2003).

"The reality of the history of science, and what is discovered, and what we call science, shows that there is no one way to do it," Thompson maintains. "If you engage kids in the process [of the scientific method], they realize that there is a way to do science at a technical level. But when you start to think about how to apply scientific inquiry in different contexts, that there are different ways of doing this, then you start to push into the substantive level."

## Engaging in Substantive Inquiry

Thompson recommends the following exercise as a means to demonstrate to teachers and students alike the open-ended nature of an investigation rooted in substantive inquiry. The directions for the exercise read,

> Some moist soil is placed inside a clear glass jar. A healthy green plant is planted in the soil. The cover is screwed on tightly. The jar is located in a window where it receives sunlight. Its temperature is maintained between 60° and 80°F. How long do you predict the plant will live? (NRC, 1996, p. 92)

This process of creating and observing what is essentially a terrarium reveals a number of preconceptions that adults and students may have about condensation and evaporation, transpiration, and photosynthesis. "Folks almost always have naïve ideas about what's going to happen to the plant. They have trouble applying all the tidbits of science that they have learned in the past to the plant's situation," Thompson says.

For example, education students typically predict that the plant will die without water but quickly reconsider that notion when water begins to form on the inside of the jar within a few days. On the other hand, students who have just studied photosynthesis wonder whether the plant will die from too much oxygen, which "leads to a whole conversation about gas exchange, and something else they hadn't thought about: that plants respire because they're made up of cells," Thompson notes. Meanwhile, teachers often get nervous with the activity's open-ended nature; they wonder whether it's OK to have something happen that they can't account for. Sometimes mold grows in the jar and kills the plant, for instance. Teachers want to know how they explain to students that plants' dying is a part of science. "The nature of the questions may vary depending on the group, but they almost always address the same topics but in different ways—and that's what scientists do," Thompson says.

Extended inquiries that develop over time and include healthy doses of observation, discussion, and reflection can involve teachers in new and deeper aspects of inquiry. But teachers often tell Thompson that they feel pressured to keep on moving from topic to topic to cover the curriculum, which makes them view an extended inquiry as overly time-consuming and even confusing. Teachers may also avoid embracing more substantive inquiry, Thompson suggests, because they "think they don't understand the connectedness of all these content ideas well enough. They don't realize that they could be covering a lot of the ground that they need to for the curriculum."

## The Inquiry Wheel: A New Model for Understanding

Most teachers haven't done scientific work outside a classroom setting. Even at the secondary level, only a minority of lucky science teachers get the opportunity to work with professional scientists as part of their training or ongoing development. For their part, unlike teachers, professional scientists aren't required to impart hundreds of years of scientific knowledge to young minds in a matter of months.

This disconnect between the realm of scientists and the realm of science teachers is the crux of the problem with teaching students how to understand and apply authentic inquiry in the classroom. Just where do "school-world" and "real-world" scientific inquiry overlap? It's an intriguing question whose answer might come in the form of a new model for describing inquiry known as the *inquiry wheel*. The inquiry wheel could offer teachers a more coherent understanding of science and enable them, in turn, to better engage their own students in the scientific enterprise. Science education researchers developed the inquiry wheel after comparing the typical five- or six-step version of scientific inquiry found in 40 science textbooks with the process of scientific inquiry as understood and practiced by research scientists. The model captures both the dynamic aspect of scientific inquiry and the differences among various scientific fields as revealed by scientists' own explanations of how they carry out their work (see Figure 1.2).

The inquiry wheel contains a central hub consisting of questions, and the process of generating and answering these questions propels the investigation through the following stages:

- Observing.
- Defining the problem.

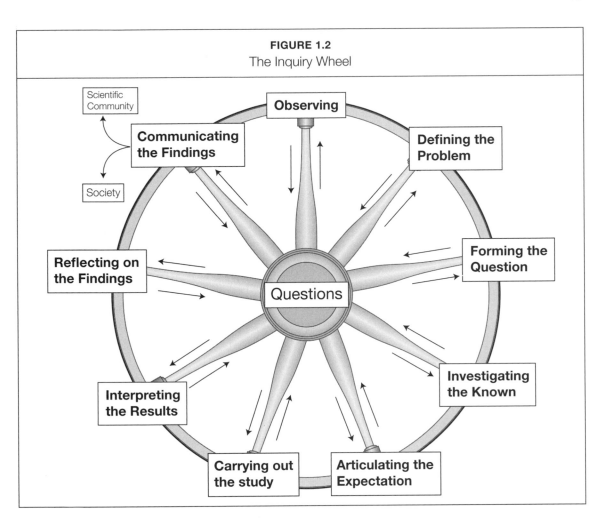

**FIGURE 1.2**
The Inquiry Wheel

- Forming the question.
- Investigating the known.
- Articulating the expectation.
- Carrying out the study.
- Interpreting the results.
- Reflecting on the findings.
- Communicating the findings to the scientific community and to society.

The dynamic relationship between the questions and the various stages of inquiry is depicted by two-way arrows (or "spokes") connecting the hub to the steps along the wheel's circumference. Generating questions at any point during the inquiry and revisiting previous stages are key elements of this model (Reiff, Harwood, & Phillipson, 2002). For example, a scientist (or student) could move from the "carrying out the study" stage back to the "observing" or "defining the problem" stage should a problem or new issue arise during an investigation.

Although the conventional steps of the scientific method and the stages on the inquiry wheel necessarily have similarities, the researchers found that scientists understand inquiry processes differently from science teachers. For example, in the classroom, the inquiry wheel's stage of "articulating the expectation" is often reduced to making predictions, typically with insufficient tools. One biologist interviewed for the inquiry wheel project lamented that students are often forced to write down predictions before they have the information they need to form a meaningful guess: "That doesn't make sense. That's not science," he asserted (Reiff et al., 2002, p. 13).

One of the textbook myths that the researchers want to dispel is that scientific inquiry inevitably leads to a theory or a law. "Even among science disciplines, scientists define hypothesis, theory, and law differently," says Hollins University education professor Rebecca Reiff, who led the study on scientists' conceptions of inquiry. For example, physicists she interviewed often used mathematical calculations or computer simulations to put forth "theories" that were really more akin to hypotheses, she says. In contrast, biologists told her that "a theory tended to develop after a lifetime of work." The role of ongoing questioning in scientific inquiry is crucial, says Reiff, noting that she "constructed the inquiry wheel to represent scientists' explanations that investigations really end in more questions."

Reiff makes a strong case that the linear depiction of the scientific method found in most textbooks "fails to accurately portray the lively process" that scientists actually use for their work. Compared with the textbook version of the scientific method, the inquiry wheel "provides a more sophisticated and more authentic model" of scientific inquiry by highlighting such aspects as reflecting on the findings, which some scientists consider the most underrated aspect of inquiry. Reiff hopes that teachers will use the inquiry wheel as a framework to help their students conceptualize the nonlinear and multidimensional processes that reflect the authentic scientific inquiry of professionals.

## Teaching Inquiry Versus Teaching Content: Finding a Balance

Science education researcher Iris Weiss acknowledges the importance of inquiry in science but notes that realistically, teachers need to strike a balance between inquiry and more traditional means of teaching. "We've made an artificial distinction between inquiry and telling. The fact that inaccessible lectures are boring and don't result in learning doesn't mean that no lectures is the best thing," she warns.

Instead, achieving the appropriate balance may depend on playing to the strengths of individual teachers. Not every science teacher may be able to lecture like the late Stephen Jay Gould, an enormously influential scientist who popularized his field in the late 20th century, but Weiss believes he was proof that one could deliver a lecture that raises questions and leads the audience to "do inquiry." Typically, Gould would raise a question and then "talk about how scientists know what they know and take you through the story line of why we thought what we used to think, and what we observed that told us otherwise," Weiss recalls from an occasion when she observed Gould. "I have seen more very capable traditional teachers turned into really lousy reformed teachers. Maybe we would have done better to allow them to do well what they did well," Weiss offers.

Use inquiry wisely, she urges: "There must be some criteria: the questions have to be something you can answer with the resources you are likely to have." Weiss evaluated one science lesson that had students spending weeks trying to figure out where earwax comes from by looking inside one another's ears. Bad choice for inquiry, Weiss says. "First of all, where earwax comes from is not a particularly thrilling and important concept. Second of all, you could look in ears from now until doomsday and never figure it out."

## Insight from the Cognitive Sciences

Research on how professionals think and work in their respective fields has led to new insights and understanding about learning in science. Science education reformers are urging teachers to make use of research within the cognitive sciences, which seek to uncover the mental processes of learning. An understanding of how learning takes place may prompt teachers to encourage more thinking in their classrooms, as opposed to "memorization and regurgitation of reading and lectures," as Robert Yager puts it.

Yager notes that this would be "a big change because high school teachers particularly look upon themselves as knowing what they need to know in order to teach. They're familiar with chemistry or biology and proceed to go through a course almost irrespective of student thought, student experiences, or student interpretations." Instead, teachers ought to be working with students to promote more energetic thinking and better understanding because those are the "basic ingredients" of science, Yager explains. According to this model, concepts, facts, and inquiry (in both its intellectual and its hands-on or sensory aspects) play mutually supportive roles in helping students to learn science.

For example, one key research finding emphasizes the importance of understanding "domain-specific conceptual frameworks." Broadly, this means that the application of such concepts as *evidence* and *change* will look different within the context, or *domain*, of science than they will within the context of another subject, such as history. Within each domain, conceptual frameworks promote organization and understanding. In science, for instance, the concept of the adaptation of species gives new meaning to what a student already knows about the characteristics of fish, birds, and mammals. In turn, the concept itself is fleshed out and enriched by the factual details of the species that students have studied (Donovan & Bransford, 2005).

In *How Students Learn: Science in the Classroom*, Donovan and Bransford (2005) distill three principles from cognitive and developmental research that can help science teachers strengthen their classroom instruction and boost their students' learning:

• Address preconceptions. First, find out what students already know.

• Know what it means to "do science." Understand how constructing knowledge in this subject may differ from constructing knowledge in other subjects.

• Use metacognitive strategies. Help students reflect on their learning process.

## Addressing Preconceptions

Students enter the classroom with their own ideas about how the world operates. These preconceptions may come from a variety of informal sources, including students' own observations. Some incomplete ideas persist as misconceptions into adulthood. One well-known study (Harvard-Smithsonian Center for Astrophysics, 1987) showed that a majority of randomly chosen Harvard University graduates, faculty, and alumni could not give correct explanations for either the change in seasons or the phases of the moon. One featured misconception held that Earth has a pronounced elliptical orbit that swings closer to the sun during summer and farther from the sun in winter. The study also revealed that such fixed personal understandings are hard to root out, even after teachers provide correct information.

Accordingly, teachers who understand the individual preconceptions that students bring to a science topic can address misunderstandings directly and thus better focus their lessons. In addition, teachers must be ready to address preconceptions that students hold about the science field itself and the procedures within it. For example, Donovan and Bransford (2005) point out that many students believe experiments are performed mainly to attain a certain outcome (an understanding comparable to Thompson's concept of *technical inquiry*), or that data correlation is itself sufficient to show a causal relationship.

## "Doing" Science

Such misconceptions about the processes of science tend to occur when the processes become ends in themselves, divorced from core concepts of science. For students to learn how to "do" science, they need to understand the roles of observation, imagination, and reasoning.

Donovan and Bransford point out that research has shown that experts in a field acquire and retain knowledge differently from novices. Experts add knowledge to their existing conceptual framework of "big ideas," which makes acquisition of new ideas or facts easier, and recall and application of knowledge more productive. Students, too, must "have a deep foundation of factual knowledge" to gain mastery in a scientific topic, which they must then link to a conceptual framework (Donovan & Bransford, 2005, p. 1).

National Science Foundation (NSF) senior program director Janice Earle finds promise in the reform efforts that highlight both scientific thinking and science's big ideas. Earle, who evaluates K–12 science education research projects, notes that if science's domain-specific thinking is a way of reasoning on the basis of evidence about the natural world, then schools need to give students opportunities to experience the natural world. "Cookbook labs" that involve step-by-step directions leading to certain outcomes don't satisfy the perennial call for inquiry-based learning in science. "Inquiry can be good, bad, or indifferent, just as curriculum or assessment can be good, bad, or indifferent," Earle asserts.

## Using Metacognitive Strategies

The third principle for effective science instruction involves teaching students to use metacognitive strategies to monitor their own thinking. Such strategies can be as simple as having students compare outcomes of an experiment or leading a class discussion that exposes students to different viewpoints on a topic. With guidance and support from skilled teachers, students will reconsider and refine their own ideas.

A metacognitive strategy called *reflective assessment* involves giving students a framework, such as a rubric, for evaluating their inquiry. For example, students may rate their understanding of the main ideas, understanding of the inquiry process, systematicness, inventiveness, careful reasoning, application of the tools of research, teamwork, and communication skills. Donovan and Bransford (2005) found that when given a reflective framework for their thinking, academically disadvantaged students in particular made significant gains.

## The Urban Achievement Gap

According to an *Education Week* report based on NAEP assessments in elementary and middle school science, many minority students in urban schools are failing to learn the basics of science, which include conducting investigations, interpreting graphs, and understanding scientific classifications (Cavanaugh, 2006). Researchers studying the vexing problem of racial and socioeconomic achievement gaps in science believe that greater attempts on the part of schools and teachers to understand students of color (especially those in poor urban areas), combined with conscious efforts to help such students make connections between their own world and the academic culture of science, can help put science education on a better footing. An increased use of the main reforms called for by the NRC's science education standards—including inquiry-based, hands-on science—will be key for engaging students typically considered at risk for poor performance in science, say experts.

## Dramatic Demographic Changes

Science teachers must also learn to deal with the changing demographics of their schools. In the coming decades, minority students will make up the majority of students in many schools—not just in big cities, where that is already often the case, but also in suburban and rural districts that are increasingly attracting new immigrants.

Overall, Hispanic students account for the largest increase in English language learners in U.S. schools, but in many urban areas and inner suburbs, student populations represent dozens of ethnic, linguistic, and cultural backgrounds that may complicate efforts to meet the academic needs of each student.

"Fifteen years ago, we had no ESL [English as a second language] population. Today we have thousands of students," says high school chemistry department chair Steven Long, who estimates that about 30 percent of the population at Rogers High School in Rogers, Arkansas, is

Hispanic. "We've had a lot of growing pains in the last 15 years," admits Long, who says science teachers, like other educators at the school, have taken part in "lots of workshops" to learn how to modify instruction to help English language learners. As a bonus, science teachers have learned that effective instruction for students with language needs—including such strategies as the use of graphics, hands-on science, and plain old clear speaking on the teacher's part—is also "good for all students." In addition, the school's language academy helps new students reach a minimum level of English proficiency, and sheltered classes enable English language learners to receive extra instruction in science.

## The Struggle for Student Literacy

The increased influx of English language learners has helped highlight the academic literacy problem in U.S. high schools. This problem manifests itself when students begin to confront the higher-level academic language of content areas like science. Steven Long calls student literacy a "huge issue." Long believes that certain societal changes, such as an increasing number of households with two working parents or with a single parent, contribute to a lack of reading at home that is a departure from households of the past. The effect of poor literacy becomes detrimental at the secondary level, where students should already be proficient in "reading to learn."

"I have many colleagues who tell me they are told to teach literacy at whatever cost: if content must be sacrificed, then sacrifice it. Literacy is what we're being measured with. It's not merely an elementary issue. It's a secondary issue," Long points out. "I don't care how you incorporate it, but I cannot teach literacy with the same speed and efficiency with which I teach content. I am not a literacy teacher—I don't have those skills. And many teachers are in the same boat." He quickly adds, "It's not wrong to teach literacy, but at the secondary level, we have to find more efficient ways of doing that so we don't sacrifice content."

# Global Competition and the Promise of Technology

The demand for "good"—even excellent—students in science is increasing. Business and industry leaders in particular are leading the charge for better science teaching so that students become tech-savvy and science-savvy adults who can fuel the economic engines of a highly technological era. These days, say those who study global trends and international competition, economic might proceeds more often than not from the ability to apply scientific and technological advances within the lucrative global marketplace.

In the report *Rising Above the Gathering Storm: Energizing and Employing America for a Brighter Economic Future*, a panel of scientists, educators, and business leaders called for a number of measures to shore up what they perceived as the United States' diminishing global stature in research in science and engineering. Among other remedies, the panel suggested that the United States

• Annually recruit 10,000 science and math teachers by offering the nation's smartest students four-year college scholarships.
• Pay for professional development for science and math teachers, including summer institutes, master's degree programs, and training for advanced placement and International Baccalaureate programs.
• Create a (voluntary) model K–12 science curriculum based on a rigorous, world-class standard. (Committee on Science, Engineering, and Public Policy, 2007)

The alarm call is being heard by science teachers.

"I tell my students they are not competing with Bentonville, Arkansas—the next town over—they're competing with Bangladesh and Beijing. Students don't understand that, and only part of the parents do," says Steven Long. Crucial for economic success will be getting students to adopt not only a global mind-set but also a vision of the future that involves imagination and change. U.S. kids may be technologically savvy, Long says, but "they don't comprehend that the job they may ultimately end up with doesn't exist now. And the technology they will be using hasn't even been thought of."

These issues are part of the larger challenge of deciding how to revamp current K–12 science programs to provide students with the knowledge and understanding they need to truly consider a career in science. Education reformers and industry experts alike consider the decreasing numbers of college graduates in science, technology, engineering, and mathematics (or STEM) careers a serious handicap to U.S. supremacy in the global economy.

"We just don't have students considering STEM careers in the numbers that we once had. If nothing else, students should at least understand the importance of science, even if they don't choose it as a career," says Linda Froschauer.

Technology could be one area where the science classroom and the real world of science careers meet. The tools of the professional scientist can be found in many of today's classrooms, whether students are testing water quality with computer probeware, using digital microscopes with projection screens, or crunching data from investigations on graphing calculators. It's common for students to use the Web as a basic research tool to gather information for science projects, but the digital revolution also allows students to query working scientists or take part in interscholastic projects that pool data on weather, insect migration, the angle of the sun, or other natural phenomena, thereby enabling students to experience the type of work that professionals do.

Although technology will not provide a panacea for every difficulty facing science education, science educators ought to be using it to help students develop "21st century skills" that will be crucial in a knowledge-based economy, say experts. These skills include digital literacy, inventive thinking, effective communication, and the ability to create high-quality products. Christopher Dede, Timothy E. Wirth Professor in Learning Technologies at Harvard's Graduate School of Education, explains that such skills enable people to resolve new problems with incomplete information, work on a diverse team (in person or remotely), and master knowledge by "filtering a sea of information" (Allen, 2001).

Just as scientists use computational models to demonstrate and visualize concepts, make estimations, analyze data, or solve problems through simulations, students now have access to similar tools through the National Science Digital Library (www.nsdl.org) and the associated Computational Science Education Reference Desk. This National Science Foundation project brings together high-quality computer-based teaching tools that can help teachers find new ways to integrate science, technology, engineering, and math.

## Rethinking High School Science: Is Integration the Answer?

Figuring out the skills that students will need for the 21st century workplace is "a big, complex issue," says Rodger Bybee, executive director of the Biological Sciences Curriculum Study (BSCS). "In science, [fostering 21st century skills] means using an inquiry orientation in classrooms. That would include having students working on semistructured problems in groups, having them think logically and critically, and having them understand the role of data in analyzing or resolving problems." He adds, "For nearly two decades, the science education community has focused efforts on K–8 reform, and we haven't really attended in a serious way to reforming and improving high schools. It's time to take a look at high school science."

This push to reconsider high school science, as well as the renewed emphasis on inquiry and conceptual understanding, has some experts reexamining the purpose of the various science disciplines. University of Iowa professor Robert Yager, a 50-year veteran of science education research, recently recalled that the emergence of separate science disciplines in U.S. high schools and colleges has been a relatively recent development. In 1892, when Harvard University began requiring physics for college entrance, high schools began putting it in their science curricula on the recommendation of the Committee of Ten, a blue-ribbon group that sought to streamline the chaotic secondary curricula of the period. Chemistry became a requirement around 1902, and biology was designated a science when zoology, botany, and various agriculture-related courses were combined around 1920 (Yager, 2006). Yager's point seems to be that the focus of separate science disciplines in high school contributes to the popular but erroneous conception that *knowing about* science is the same as *doing* science. "As we think of change and reform, we must define science achievement in terms of all the qualities and facets of science itself and resist defining it as 'information known to scientists' that all high school graduates should also know," Yager asserted (2006, p. 10).

Rodger Bybee cites the "Physics First" movement as one example of how science educators are trying to rethink the high school science curriculum. Physics First science programs, which tend to be adopted by smaller schools and districts, reorder the sequence of secondary science from the century-old biology-chemistry-physics to physics-chemistry-biology. Advocates of the Physics First curriculum say it makes conceptual sense to introduce the elements of physics as early as 8th grade because it lays a good foundation for more advanced science courses in high school. The movement's supporters also claim that making physics a requirement early in high school exposes a significantly larger number of students to the subject.

Another curricular model seeking to expose students to more branches of science in high school makes use of the coordinated science approach. BSCS is currently developing *BSCS Science: An Inquiry Approach*, a standards-based science curriculum for grades 9–11. Each year of the curriculum begins with an overarching unit focusing on different aspects of the inquiry process, including the role of questions and concepts (9th grade); the process of designing investigations (10th grade); and evidence as the explanation for models (11th grade). Then, at each grade level, students cover three eight-week core units devoted to physical science, life science, and earth and space science. Each unit includes initial lessons focusing on science concepts as well as an integrating chapter that ties these concepts to the natural world (Bybee, 2006). In the 9th grade physical science unit, for example, students link what they have learned about the properties of matter and atomic structure to the creation of various colors of fireworks when metallic compounds are burned. A final unit ties concepts to topics relevant to students' lives, such as global warming, in a way that helps students integrate those concepts across the disciplines, Bybee says.

"By then, students have ample opportunity to really develop the concepts that they need from the three basic disciplines in order to understand the problem," he notes. "I think it's important that many districts recognize that they have to teach some physical science as well as life and earth sciences across the grades."

How best to juggle and teach the science disciplines has been a perennial problem facing schools, and there has been no shortage of solutions. Yet for all the similarities between today's curriculum and the curriculum of the late 19th century, Charles Eliot might be surprised if he were alive today to find that many of the Committee of Ten's recommendations have yet to be fully realized, despite continual reform efforts during the last 100 years. For elementary school, Eliot's blue-ribbon panel envisioned a daily science period and a science specialist to help primary teachers; for secondary school, the committee called for students to spend 60 percent of their science classes engaging in lab work, advocated the use of lab notebooks, and advised both written and lab-based science assessments. For both elementary and secondary students, the committee "dwells repeatedly on the importance of the study of things and phenomena by direct contact" (National Education Association [NEA], 1893, p. 26). It all sounds utterly fresh—and eerily familiar. The latest reform movement started by the NRC's *National Science Education Standards*—a relatively young 11 years old given the long history of science reform—is really just beginning.

## Reflections  ◆  ◆  ◆

As the excesses of the Information Age bring home the reality that scientific knowledge continues to amass at an astonishing rate, history shows us that science educators have always sought better ways to help students corral that knowledge into a coherent understanding of science. These efforts have unintentionally produced a pendulum effect during the last century, with the focus alternating between rigor and relevance. Today, secondary science is poised to find a better balance between these two principles, with its renewed emphasis on authentic inquiry and mastering the big ideas within the science disciplines. Secondary science reforms are revving up once again, some in an effort to meet NCLB's accountability measures, others in opposition to them. As science educators figure out ways to ensure that their students have truly mastered science concepts and processes, they need to reassess how they do business in the classroom. The following chapters show how teachers and school administrators are managing the latest call for science education reform.

# Planning a Curriculum of Essentials

2

*Happy is he who is able to understand the causes of things.*

—*Virgil*

A recent study of science standards in 49 U.S. states found 22 of them far below par, earning a grade of *D* or *F* for being too long and hard to navigate and for missing essential science concepts, among other problems. Nine more states earned a mediocre *C* (Thomas B. Fordham Institute, 2005).

Faced with lengthy, unwieldy state science standards, curriculum administrators and teachers are overwhelmed by the apparent demand to teach massive quantities of science content and skills. Science education reformers believe that the best way for school districts to deal with these demands is to carefully select the most important standards to teach. This is easier said than done, however, considering the fact that large-scale science assessments tend to test what is easily measured: discrete facts, formulas, and procedures. The big science concepts often get lost in the dust of factoids and vocabulary definitions.

George Nelson, director of science, mathematics, and technology education at Western Washington University, describes a typical standards-based unit on the cell: a student sees "a big picture of this flat thing that's supposed to be a cell. It has 20 different little gizmos inside—and the student has to memorize terms like *endoplasmic reticulum*, *golgi bodies*, *nucleus*, and all the other pieces that are there," says Nelson, who is also a past director of Project 2061, a science education reform group that has taken commercial publishers to task for marketing confusing, overly crammed science textbooks.

What's important, argues Nelson—and what is emphasized at the national level by such publications as *National Science Educations Standards* and *Benchmarks for Science Literacy*—is the overarching concept "that the cell is the basic unit of life and carries out all the same functions that life does" with the help of subunits within the cell. These functions help the cell fulfill its need for food, water, and air—the same needs of all living organisms. "Learning the names of all these parts of the cell—which is often the main learning goal now—is irrelevant. What's important is how life works."

To improve science teaching in the short term, science education expert Rodger Bybee recommends that curriculum directors carry out horizontal (grade-level) and vertical (cross-grade) analyses of their curricula "to bring greater coherence to the program they've got." To help science educators identify and teach essential concepts that can be articulated and developed across grade levels, many school districts and research-based curriculum writers are looking to a curriculum approach known as *backward design*.

## The Case for Backward Design

In their book *Understanding by Design* (2005), Grant Wiggins and Jay McTighe make the case that backward design can correct the excesses of what they call the "twin sins" of traditional curriculum design. The first sin embraces an activity-oriented curriculum that offers engaging, "hands-on" experiences that nonetheless lack an explicit focus on important ideas. Teachers committing the second sin—"coverage"—make a heroic attempt to march students through a curriculum or a textbook within a prescribed period of time, focusing mostly on memorizing facts.

In contrast to these approaches, backward design "begins with the end in mind, and designs toward that end" (Wiggins & McTighe, 2005, p. 338). Backward design consists of three stages:

**1. Identify desired results.** Review teaching goals, content standards, and curriculum expectations. Then prioritize these by focusing on what students ought to know, understand, and be able to do within the framework of "big ideas."

**2. Determine acceptable evidence of achieving desired results.** Evidence can include summative assessments, such as end-of-teaching tests and culminating tasks, and formative assessments, such as quizzes, performance tasks, projects, observations, and student self-assessments.

**3. Plan learning experiences and instruction.** Make appropriate choices about teaching methods, lesson sequence, and resource materials with the aim of guiding students to perform effectively (stage 2) and to achieve the desired results (stage 1).

## Stage 1: Identifying Desired Results

In practice, determining the desired results of a given unit requires several components, notes John Brown, author of *Making the Most of Understanding by Design* (2004). First, curriculum writers should separate the standards into two categories: (1) those that students need to gain a deep understanding of the subject—the so-called *power standards*; and (2) other kinds of knowledge that students should already grasp or at least be familiar with. Power standards yield the *big ideas*, which may be conceptual patterns, themes, processes, perspectives, or universal issues. Curriculum writers use a unit's big ideas to draw up statements of *enduring understandings* that delineate each idea's details and points of inquiry. The final step is to write *essential questions* to provoke student inquiry, investigation, and debate of the big ideas. These essential questions can be framed with such prompts as "How . . . ?", "Why . . . ?", and "To what extent . . . ?" These essential questions should be carefully written, taking into account the grade level and the specific requirements or goals of the unit being studied.

Enduring understandings and essential questions enable students to maintain their focus on big ideas and the connections among them and thereby to deepen their learning within the discipline or unit. According to Brown (2004), "students develop deep conceptual understanding when they can cue into the enduring understandings and essential questions at the heart of their curriculum. Enduring understandings are statements that clearly articulate big ideas that have lasting value beyond the classroom and that students can revisit throughout their lives. Essential questions are big, open-ended interpretive questions that have no one obvious right answer. They raise other important questions, recur naturally, and go to the heart of a discipline or content area's philosophical and conceptual foundations."

Brown points out that state and district standards often contain enduring understandings, either overtly or implicitly. However, he cautions, because state standards tend to be numerous and lengthy, educators may find it difficult to identify power standards containing the specific language that can help them pinpoint enduring understandings and essential questions. In such cases, educators have to "unpack" the big ideas and articulate the enduring understandings themselves.

When high school biology teacher Elvia Solis led an ASCD workshop titled Understanding by Design in the Secondary Science Classroom, she worked with teachers of earth science, physics, and biology to identify some of the enduring understandings and essential questions behind big ideas that are found in the main science disciplines. Among the enduring understandings they arrived at were the following:

- All organisms change over time.
- Patterns exist in the world around us.
- Mass and energy are neither created nor destroyed.
- Measures are essential to the continuation of scientific advancement.

Working out the enduring understandings can be hard, says Solis, because "they're not so obvious and people tend to argue over them." When she conducts backward design sessions at Arlington High School in inner-city Indianapolis, Solis and other teachers embark on the first step of the three-stage backward design process by deciding which state science standards they "must absolutely include" as the power standards.

For example, to launch the design of an earth science unit on fossils and geologic time, Solis focuses on three performance indicators tied to

Indiana's two overarching science standards that address the principles of a particular science discipline and the historical perspectives within it:

**ES.1.28:** Discuss geologic evidence, including fossils and radioactive dating, in relation to Earth's past.

**ES.1.29:** Recognize and explain that in geologic change, the present arises from the materials of the past in ways that can be explained according to the same physical and chemical laws.

**ES.2.5:** Explain that the idea that Earth might be vastly older than most people believed made little headway in science until the work of Lyell and Hutton. (Indiana Department of Education, 2006)

Because these three performance indicators have been selected as power standards, the unit's enduring understandings can be expressed using the standards' actual language. For example, the enduring understanding for ES.1.29 might be phrased as follows: "Students will understand that in geologic change, the present arises from the materials of the past in ways that can be explained according to the same physical and chemical laws." Essential questions developed to address this standard might include "How can present geologic changes be explained according to physical and chemical laws?" and "To what extent do all current geologic changes arise from the materials of the past?"

## Stage 2: Determining Acceptable Evidence of Achieving Desired Results

During this stage, Solis and the other science teachers choose or develop a variety of assessments linked to the standards and big ideas designated in the first stage. Specifically, the teachers want to assess students on how well they understand fossils and geologic time.

For the unit's performance assessment, Solis asks students to role-play as geologists who need to examine the layers of rocks below a property on which a company wants to build an in-ground stadium. Students are given "core samples" from the rock that they use to identify and diagram the various layers of rock and determine their ages based on the fossils within. The assessment activity also has students sort and label fossils by type (e.g., mold, cast, trace); by animal or plant name;

and by geologic time (e.g., Devonian, Jurassic). Through this activity, students should be able to demonstrate that they know what fossils are, where they can be found, and how they are formed, Solis explains. Other assessments ask students to show that they understand radioactive dating and the theories of 18th century naturalist James Hutton and 19th century geologist Charles Lyell, both of whom countered the scientific thinking of their day by suggesting that Earth's present land formation took place slowly, over vast periods of time.

At this stage, teachers also develop other forms of assessment that will reveal students' learning. For example, formative assessment devices—such as journal entries, responses to prompts, data collection, diagrams, and questions that students have posed and researched answers for—provide evidence that helps teachers to make instructional decisions during the unit. During this stage, teachers also determine the use of quizzes, textbook tests, vocabulary lists, and study aids.

## Stage 3: Planning Learning Experiences and Instruction

During the third stage, teachers develop a variety of small-group and lab activities. As an introductory activity to answer the question "What is a fossil?", students look at samples of fossils, then form small groups to share their prior knowledge of fossils and discuss a list of terms related to paleontology and geologic history. For homework, students are to use 10 vocabulary words to create a quiz, trading cards, or a crossword puzzle, thus familiarizing themselves with the new terms.

Lab activities for the unit give students hands-on experiences examining and identifying fossils. For example, students armed with magnifying glasses or stereoscopes identify objects in a box as fossils, human artifacts, or "something else," then offer a justification for their conclusions, Solis explains. Another lab activity gives students the tools to create fossil models, such as trace fossils of animal tracks, cast fossils, and mold fossils of shell pieces, chicken feet, or other objects chosen from nature. To create their own "prehistoric amber," students heat corn syrup to its boiling point to evaporate much of the water and then insert an insect into the remaining corn syrup, which hardens as it cools.

During another lab Solis describes, students examine the school's "boxes and boxes of fossils" to analyze and identify different fossils' types and originating organisms. Students also write explanations about the geologic changes of the land that brought about the final location of certain fossils, such as the seashell fossils found on mountaintops, which puzzled scientists hundreds of years ago.

For extra credit, students may conduct research to create a time line for a common animal (such as a horse, a hippopotamus, or a bird), including drawings or pictures from the Internet to show changes in particular features, such as hooves, over the eons.

## The Bottom Line on Backward Design

Solis believes that backward design's logic of "starting with the goal" has commonsense appeal to teachers and makes the curriculum clearer to teachers and students alike. The model enables teachers to inform students up front what they'll be expected to know and do, Solis notes, so students "give focus to the class activities while we're doing them."

In the new forensic chemistry course at Arlington High, for example, students know from the start that the final project will involve simulating and analyzing a crime scene, so all the study, work, and activities in the course support this culminating project. "Students are paying attention—they're getting involved," Solis says. According to urban science teachers, this level of engagement is unusual at urban schools with dominantly minority student bodies (at Arlington, 97 percent of students are minorities, and 80 percent are eligible for free or reduced-price lunch).

Solis notes that there are challenges to backward design, especially when curriculum units run from three to four weeks long. "I've had to dispense with some fun activities. If I evaluate them right, I realize the labs may have been fun, but they were not addressing the understanding that I want my students to have," she explains. This is exactly what backward design is supposed to do: steer curriculum and instruction away from the "sins" of dead-end activities and content cramming.

Although Solis has not collected data on whether backward design increases achievement, she does know that students make more connections between big ideas and related information that they come across outside school. One year, Solis designed a hydrology unit that she kicked off with the provocative question "Where did all the dinosaur urine go?" to pique student interest in the water cycle. It worked: after the school year ended, a student returned to tell her that her lessons fit into his summer job testing water quality for a local utility.

Using backward design also leads Solis to develop lessons more consciously, keeping in mind both the goals of the unit and her students' array of abilities. When she's deciding classroom activities in stage 3, for example, Solis sometimes catches herself favoring language skills activities, so she then reconfigures the activities to include some that address alternative learning styles or appeal to a variety of multiple intelligences.

## Backward Design Meets Lesson Study

When Pennsylvania's Neshaminy School District decided to overhaul its science curriculum, teachers used backward design to develop "pretty rigorous units of study," according to Robert Kolenda, the district's K–12 science coordinator. Kolenda emphasizes that "using backward design makes teachers more self-reflective about what they're teaching and why they're teaching it. They get better at understanding what the big ideas [of a unit or discipline] are and why they're worth learning."

To further hone Neshaminy's backward-designed curriculum units, Kolenda has introduced *lesson study* format. Widely used in Japan, lesson study involves teachers collaboratively developing a lesson and then observing its implementation in the classroom. Following the observation, the group offers a critique and suggests refinements. After the teacher revises the lesson, the group observes it again to check whether it meets the goals the group sought for it.

Whereas backward design gets teachers to define the big ideas of the unit, lesson study gives teachers a chance to fine-tune the instruction of one particular lesson in that unit. Typically, a team of teachers will spend one to two days developing a unit and another day having one team member demonstrate the lesson in the classroom while a team of two to four teachers observes. For example, for a unit on the characteristics and behavior of water, teachers agreed that water's behavior as a polar molecule, its cohesive and adhesive properties, and its capillary action were essential content to teach students. Then, using a lesson study protocol, teachers examined a particular lesson that addressed water's cohesive and adhesive properties.

The five-column lesson study protocol used by Kolenda's district is a graphic organizer that shows the teaching team

1. How the lesson is segmented from start to finish, with approximate duration times.

2. Expectations of students during these segments.

3. Common student misconceptions and how they will be addressed.

4. "Points to notice," or factors the team will focus on during the demonstration lesson (e.g., engagement of students with learning disabilities).

5. The materials and instructional strategies needed for each segment of the lesson.

On the day of the water properties lesson teachers observe one member of their team teach the lesson and then meet afterward for the critique. If possible, another team member may teach the revised lesson the same day, Kolenda says. "When we get the lesson where we want it," he continues, the lesson study team meets with other colleagues at an after-school workshop to share the unit they developed with backward design, the research lesson, and copies of all the materials so that anyone can incorporate them into his or her instruction.

Using backward design's stage 2 helped teachers "think like the assessor," which dovetailed with another district initiative to infuse more performance assessments into their teaching practice. For example, the old approach for teaching and assessing the concept of osmosis in 10th grade biology had teachers directing students in a cookbook lab, supplied with a set question to investigate, a list of procedures, fill-in-the-blank data tables, and follow-up questions. Now, the performance assessment on osmosis requires students to design the experiment so that the onus of the learning process is on them. "As a result, students are problem solving and thinking more deeply about what they are doing because they need to come up with a list of materials and the procedures, and they need to find a way to communicate their findings as well as write the conclusion," Kolenda says. "Could we improve our performance assessments? Certainly. But we're light-years ahead of where we were."

Revamping the curriculum to focus on important science concepts has been an ongoing, sometimes grueling, process carried out in the summer and during the school year with the help of Title II funds for professional development. But the effort should have students better prepared for the NCLB-mandated science testing to be taken by 4th, 8th, and 11th grade students. Kolenda has learned that about half of the Pennsylvania State Science Assessment will test students on such science process skills as recognizing variables and controlling them in a designed experiment, interpreting data, and measuring correctly.

Kolenda plans on gathering student achievement data on a regular basis after the state science assessments begin. He believes the data will give him the evidence to show the benefits to teaching and learning that backward design offers. "I find it one of the easiest ways to use for organizing curriculum that consistently gives us a good product," Kolenda affirms.

## Looking Ahead to Learning Progressions

As crucial to science education reform as the development and publication of *National Science Education Standards* and *Benchmarks for Science Literacy* (published by the American Association for the Advancement of Science in 1993) have been, many science education experts admit that such publications still require coverage of too many standards. In their estimation, most state science frameworks fare even worse in that regard.

Education researcher Iris Weiss, who formerly taught high school biology, highlights the peril of demanding the same standards over and over again throughout middle school and high school: "Seventh grade life science was a watered-down version of 10th grade biology. And 10th grade biology was a watered-down version of introductory college biology.

So by the time kids came to you in 10th grade, they were familiar enough with biology to be bored but not familiar enough with it to actually know the content."

Education researchers like Weiss hope that *learning progressions*, which help to streamline and connect science concepts within and across grade levels, will give "priority and coherence" to more powerful content.

For example, to understand the concepts of matter and atomic molecular theory, students at the elementary school level should first understand that the physical world around them consists of material that can be described, measured, and classified according to its properties. Next, they learn that such matter can be transformed—but not created or destroyed—by chemical and physical processes, such as digestion, decay, or erosion.

In middle school, the students build on these earlier notions and move their understanding to the molecular level. They learn that matter consists of atoms bound together into molecules, which determine the properties of the material; that such properties can alter due to both changes and underlying continuity in the atoms and molecules; and, finally, that the properties of atomic and molecular transformations are distinguished from the physical changes that occur (Wilson & Bertenthal, 2005). This learning progression takes into account the development of students' thinking as it moves from the concrete to the abstract, an important capacity for understanding atomic-molecular theory (Smith, Wiser, Anderson, Krajcik, & Coppola, 2004).

The simple logic of learning progressions—focus on essential aspects of a scientific concept and introduce it in developmentally appropriate stages—would seem to lend itself to districts revamping their own curricula with such in mind, but Weiss warns against teachers and districts taking on these tasks themselves.

For one thing, science education experts believe that more research is necessary to determine the age-appropriate introduction of material recommended by standards documents (Smith et al., 2004). "This notion that teachers should be developing their own materials is a little bit like telling doctors that they should do their own medical research—it doesn't make sense," Weiss says. Teachers have neither the time nor the expertise to develop their own learning progressions, she says. "I think we have a lot of romantic notions in our profession that everything has to be tailored to the needs of a particular group of kids. That sounds great, except for the little bit of research we have showing that when teachers modify their instructional materials, they make them worse."

Instead, Weiss argues, teachers should be rewarded for competent implementation of high-quality instructional materials. Then teachers could focus their energies on ensuring that particular groups of students, such as underachievers, really understand the concepts. But there is one problem, Weiss admits: there's just not much research-based, high-quality instructional material available for high school science. While noting that the National Science Foundation is funding research to develop curriculum materials with learning progressions, mostly at the middle school level, Weiss notes that the NSF has not funded many curriculum projects at the high school level. "In part, it's a kind of despair about what decent materials would look like because there is a huge amount of content to cover," she notes.

High school teachers get caught in the middle, Weiss concedes. They are "stuck between the press of what hasn't been addressed in the lower grades, and what the kids are expected to know in order to go on to college science." Weiss points to the advanced placement science curriculum that shoulders the heavy requirements of what colleges expect high school graduates to know.

"It's hard to know how much of it is because of expectations and how much is because we've sold teachers what I believe is a false bill of goods that says, 'If you don't develop your own materials, somehow you're not a full professional,'" Weiss speculates. She thinks that this challenge is sending the wrong message to teachers because it defies the amount of time and available expertise typical high school teachers have to draw on, especially if they're tasked to teach more than one branch of science. "If they're well trained in one, then more than likely they're not well trained in another," Weiss suggests. Writing high-quality curriculum takes an enormous amount of time, she points out.

Rather than having teachers develop their own learning progressions, Weiss says that the best way to get high-quality instructional materials into the schools is to disseminate research to commercial publishers and then get states to demand it through their curriculum adoption processes. That will give publishers an incentive to change how they do business, Weiss contends. "That's the only way to infuse it into the regular instruction materials. Publishers are not going to spend money unless they have to," she says.

## Reflections ◆ ◆ ◆

Faced with a welter of science standards, the three-stage process of backward design of curriculum can help science educators target and delve deeply into so-called big ideas to help their students gain deeper conceptual understandings within the branches of science. Focusing on big ideas also enables districts to better articulate learning objectives across grade levels. However, because big ideas often rest on other big ideas and prior knowledge, a map of the progression of prior understandings can also help teachers deepen student understanding about important concepts without getting bogged down by secondary factoids that can divert students from essential concepts. Although this approach is promising, much research remains to be done on the creation and use of such learning progressions in the classroom.

# 3

# Bringing the Curriculum to Life in the Classroom

*What I am going to tell you about is what we teach our physics students in the third or fourth year of graduate school. . . . It is my task to convince you not to turn away because you don't understand it. You see, my physics students don't understand it. . . . That is because I don't understand it. Nobody does.*

—Richard Feynman

## Fidelity Versus Innovation

In science education circles, there's an ongoing debate about where the curriculum ends and the teacher begins as *the* magic ingredient to energize and engage students, to help them grasp science deeply, and to increase their achievement. Of course the answers are complex, but the mediocre state of secondary-level science achievement has science educators and researchers worried. Students' years in middle school and high school are crucial: their experiences in science class could either awaken and stimulate their further interest in college science and science careers or convince them that they "can't do" science.

This chapter examines both sides of the teacher-versus-curriculum conundrum. While weighted toward those innovative and exemplary teachers whom all students dream of having and who receive public recognition for their talent and hard work, the chapter begins with new research showing that a well-written standards-based science curriculum, when faithfully adhered to, can also make a difference in student learning and achievement.

## Keeping the Faith with a High-Quality Curriculum

Scaling up Curriculum for Achievement, Learning, and Equity Project, or SCALE-uP (www.gwu.edu/~scale-up), is a massive five-year research project that studied the effect of three standards-based science units on science achievement in a diverse student population. Project investigators, who conducted research in Maryland's Montgomery County Public Schools, found that students from a variety of racial, ethnic, and socio-economic backgrounds learned science more effectively when teachers used highly rated, hands-on curricula and were faithful to teaching them as their developers had intended.

Sharon Lynch, professor of secondary education at George Washington University in Washington, D.C., is principal investigator of SCALE-uP. Lynch mounted the project because she wanted to test whether giving minority students challenging resources ought to be the starting point for answering questions about equity in science education. Lynch says other research has shown that curriculum materials might need to be adapted for different ethnicities—but she is skeptical.

"What's kind of driven me crazy personally is that you would have to adapt things for children before you would give them the good resources and tools to begin with. A lot of times, there are kids who are disadvantaged by the system, and you see this achievement gap. So the assumption is 'they can't do it.' But if you look a little harder, you see that they don't have the best materials, or the lab equipment, or the best teachers," Lynch points out.

Lynch and her colleagues chose three units for middle school students based on their high rankings according to a Project 2061 rating scale for science curricula: AIRES-Exploring Motion and Forces: Speed, Acceleration, and Friction (6th grade); The Real Reason for the Seasons (7th grade); and Chemistry That Applies (8th grade). Two of the three units that were studied have since been "scaled up" and are being taught in all the district's 38 middle schools, reaching 11,000 8th graders and, initially, 8,000 6th graders.

Researchers and science educators believe the evidence shows that the use of these units—one on chemistry and the other on motions and forces—will continue to have a positive influence on student science achievement even after the program is rolled out to all students and teachers. One reason is that these kinds of research-based curricula, referred to as "integrated instructional units" in the National Research Council's *America's Lab Report: Investigations in High School Science*, carefully link lab experiences with a variety of learning activities, including lectures, readings, and discussions that reinforce the target concepts of the lesson (Singer, Hilton, & Schweingruber, 2006, p. 82).

"These units were scaffolded in a fashion that made sense to students, whereas average teachers putting a unit together themselves may be missing critical pieces that are important for kids to really learn the science," says Bonnie Hansen-Grafton, an instructional specialist for science in Montgomery County Public Schools and a co–principal investigator in charge of the district's involvement in SCALE-uP.

Over the course of the project, the team of researchers from George Washington University has pinpointed the factors that make two of the three experimental curriculum units effective in helping students make sense of the science concepts. These units

• Scaffold the lesson's concepts and the use of its instructional strategies.

• Provide opportunities for student-to-student discourse.

• Give students time both to carry out the investigation and to raise and answer their own questions without receiving the answers from teachers.

• Give students thinking and writing opportunities before, during, and after the investigation, enabling them to explore preconceptions, wrestle with data and conclusions, and think through how their own conceptions have changed.

• Structure lessons so that students focus on understanding the concept rather than on merely defining vocabulary.

**Scaffolding concepts and instructional strategies.** In the 8th grade unit Chemistry That Applies, students grasp the law of the conservation of matter by exploring the chemical reactions of burning butane, rusting iron, decomposing water, and combining baking soda with vinegar. Bonnie Hansen-Grafton likes to explain the scaffolding aspect of this successful science curriculum as "hitting the concept a minimum of three times and in three different ways."

For example, students start out by mixing substances and making general observations of the results. They then revisit the experiment and make more detailed observations to distinguish mixtures from chemical reactions. They repeat the experiment again, this time quantifying the chemical reactions to determine whether mass is conserved. Finally, they build atomic models to depict the bonding that occurred in the chemical reactions, using toothpicks and colored gumdrops that represent elements such as oxygen and carbon.

The variety of activities within the investigation enable students to observe variations in the concept of change in the states of matter shown by the chemical reactions (i.e., solid to solid, liquid to solid, and liquid to gas). "They didn't do just one experiment to demonstrate the conservation of matter—they tried to demonstrate it in all the modalities," Hansen-Grafton points out. Teachers did complain that the lesson seemed to "go over the same thing over and over and over," she recalls. Yet in reviewing the pre-test and post-test scores and interviewing students about what they had learned, researchers found that students got a much wider understanding of conservation of matter than did students who hadn't participated in the same unit.

In fact, the variety of activities appeal to students' different learning styles. "Some kids are really into the manipulation of the equipment and writing down data. Other kids sit back until the end and then try to analyze what happened. And other kids are more willing to talk and chat about it. Students don't just do experiments, and then that's the end of it," Hansen-Grafton says. Instead, they talk to one another about the experiments, raise questions, and adjust and redo the investigation. Giving students opportunities to discuss and revisit their investigation provides *multiple modalities*, or multiple ways to access and manipulate the information cognitively, Hansen-Grafton points out. The fact that students have relevant, concrete experiences to draw on as they are introduced to new ideas enhances their learning. These same experiences are also useful to challenge their preconceptions about what happens when certain substances are mixed.

**Providing opportunities for student-to-student discourse.** The researchers found that English language learners and students with learning disabilities particularly benefit from the informal peer discussion that occurs during investigations—"even if they're not the ones talking," Hansen-Grafton notes. The most successful curriculum materials provide appropriate questions to guide students in discussions, she emphasizes. In the Chemistry That Applies unit, for example, the provided questions lead students to talk about whether the mixtures and reactions of substances caused changes in their mass, and "what it means" if the mass increased, decreased, or stayed the same.

**Giving students time to set up and carry out the investigation.** The successful science units in the study provide plenty of time for students to conduct their investigations and to raise and puzzle through questions about their activity. Ideally, even when students call on the teacher with questions, he or she asks them other questions instead of supplying ready-made answers.

Among the teachers of the three dozen middle schools in the study, those with block schedules had the luxury of more discussion time with their students, but they also complained that it took too long to teach a unit because they had science only every other day. "Time is an issue when your schedule is jam-packed. It comes back to depth-versus-breadth of the curriculum and making choices about what's really important to teach—the big concepts," Hansen-Grafton says. But even if it takes time, teaching different aspects of the big concepts in multiple ways enhances student achievement, she adds.

**Giving students thinking and writing opportunities before, during, and after the investigation.** To get students in the Chemistry That

Applies unit to recognize and reflect on their preconceptions about the conservation of mass, the teacher assigns them a prewriting exercise to think out the following: Will folded laundry weigh more than a pile of laundry?

During the experiment following the prewriting exercise, students weigh a single object in different forms, such as steel wool balled up and spread out. Before weighing the steel wool both ways, students talk and write about what they think would make the steel wool weigh more as a ball.

At the end of the experiment, "when hopefully the two ended up weighing the same"—not always guaranteed in middle schools, laughs Hansen-Grafton—students grapple with the writing prompt, "How did that change your thinking?" Putting such discrepant events—those that tend to surprise students' expectations—before students as a stimulus to think about their preconceptions gives students plenty of fodder to write about and helps generate new questions to explore. However, what's important is not the quantity of writing, Hansen-Grafton cautions, but that students return to the original question and document how their thinking changed.

**Structuring lessons so that students focus on understanding the concept rather than on merely defining vocabulary.** Linguistic anthropologists involved in SCALE-uP analyzed videotapes of student interaction that provide interesting insight into how the structure of the science lessons, with their emphasis on discussion and exploration, fosters conceptual understanding. Students' concrete experiences with science phenomena enable them more easily to understand and talk about new concepts (DeBoer, 1991). In fact, the researchers found that the students devised their own terms to help them communicate with one another while they learned the science concepts or worked with new processes in the labs. For example, in the chemistry unit, some students coined the terms *before-weight* and *after-weight* to designate the weight of substances before and after a chemical reaction.

Researchers say that such creation of terms is a way to deal with physical phenomena—that, in essence, students are grappling with concepts by naming them. The invented language allows students, like scientists, to "talk science." As they coin these informal terms, students show a sophisticated way of using language that indicates their understanding of what is happening, Sharon Lynch suggests.

## The Importance of Fidelity

SCALE-uP did encounter a few hitches. When the 6th grade unit on motion and forces failed to repeat its initial success in subsequent years, puzzled researchers decided not to scale up. Instead, they and science teachers reviewed the project data, including videos of classroom lessons using the unit.

What they found intrigued them. To save money, the county had sought permission from the curriculum publisher to make photocopies of the unit's student notebook and its guiding questions to distribute to students as handouts. As a result, "kids were getting pages in dribs and drabs. They didn't have a notebook; they had pieces of a notebook—and these are 6th graders," Lynch points out, suggesting that the many handouts were at risk of getting lost.

For the following year of the study, students were each given their own notebook. "We wanted to make sure that we were implementing the unit with fidelity before we said that it wasn't working," Lynch notes. "And fidelity implies that each child has his or her own notebook." The same year, researchers also sent observers into the classrooms to measure how faithfully teachers were implementing the lessons. "When we got the results, they were terrific," Lynch recalls with some relief. "For groups of kids that schools would be most worried about—English language learners, kids eligible for free and reduced meals, minorities—the effect of the treatment group outperformed the comparison group."

## What Didn't Work

Although the 6th and 8th grade science units implemented as part of SCALE-uP were found to be effective, the 7th grade unit, titled The Real Reason for the Seasons, did not fare as well. As a result, it was not scaled up in Montgomery County's 7th grade science classes.

A number of drawbacks to the unit arose in the study, notes Bonnie Hansen-Grafton. For example, instead of having teachers elicit students' own preconceptions on the causes of the changing seasons, the unit had teachers explain common misconceptions (e.g., the idea that Earth in its orbit veers farther away from the sun during the winter and moves closer during the summer). Hansen-Grafton points out, "If too much time is spent on these incorrect ideas, students at this level become confused by those ideas and do not have a clear picture of the true science behind the phenomena." She also believes that the unit failed to meet the "three-hit" threshold for scaffolding concepts. "Hitting ideas once and moving on is not enough for middle school students—some get it, but a majority may not," she says. Another missing piece was the lack of probing questions and small-group student discussion. "Teacher-directed activities are OK once in a while, but not for the entire unit," Hansen-Grafton says.

In contrast, researchers found that teachers in the comparison group—those without the innovative unit—used a variety of curriculum materials, ranging from Web resources to episodes of *Bill Nye the Science Guy* to traditional textbooks and county-produced science guides. The teachers in the comparison group were making up their own units, but they weren't doing traditional, teacher-centered activities.

## Curriculum Matters—But Teachers Matter More

Although final reports on the SCALE-uP study are pending as of this writing, Sharon Lynch believes that the project can confirm for science educators that curriculum materials "really do matter." She notes, "They may help to some degree to level the playing field."

Although veteran teachers may be right when they say they can do as well as or better than the highly rated curriculum units that were the subject of study, Lynch believes that the evidence of the study already shows that with a really well-prepared curriculum unit, you get "a better bump" in achievement when you examine results for individual groups of students instead of analyzing performance in aggregate.

Ultimately, however, student learning relies on the teacher's ability to work with students to lead them to understanding, adds Lynch: "If kids are sitting in the lab and doing the work and not reaching the conclusions that the lab was intending them to reach, because they are children—and these science concepts are not necessarily so obvious—it's the teacher who pulls the children together and has a discussion that helps bring them to the point. That's important—it's not just this magic formula about getting the kids to work in labs. These curricula are by no means 'teacher-proof'—they take a talented teacher and a hardworking one."

## Life Science with Dat Le

Creative and hardworking science teachers know how to engage their students in ways that make the most of local resources. Dat Le teaches 7th grade life science and biology at H. B. Woodlawn, a diverse secondary school in Arlington, Virginia, that attracts independent-minded students who want some control over their education.

### Insects and the Environment

In 2006, Le won the Gustav Ohaus Award for Innovations in Science Teaching for his project titled Entomology on the East Coast, which used insects as pollutant indicators to determine the human effect on the local Chesapeake Bay watershed.

Le and his students relied on the fact that the presence or absence of certain insects and invertebrates can reveal the environmental health of different types of regions. He developed the course so that his students could have hands-on, out-of-class experiences to reinforce the following life science concepts:

• Organisms both cooperate and compete in ecosystems.

• Living organisms have the capacity to produce populations of infinite size, but environments and resources are finite.

• Humans modify ecosystems as a result of population growth, technology, and consumption. The destruction of habitats through direct harvesting, pollution, atmospheric changes, and other factors is threatening global stability, and if it is not addressed, ecosystems will be irreversibly affected.

During the investigation, students learned to use a variety of entomology instruments. They used aerial nets, field nets, and aquatic nets to trap insects in 10 different watershed sites in the Northern Virginia–Washington, D.C., area. They also used killing jars and a Berlese Apparatus, a funnel that traps insects in soil. They learned how to use spreading boards to preserve the shape of fragile insect wings and then classified, labeled, and mounted insects using pins and insect boxes.

Based on their collection of insects, students developed hypotheses about the health of the watershed and then tested their predictions using water and soil tests. For example, when students discovered that certain invertebrates, such as caddis fly, stonefly, and mayfly nymphs, were plentiful or scarce in the streams and rivers that they monitored, they tested their hypotheses about water conditions by testing for concentrations of phosphates and nitrates and low amounts of dissolved oxygen. Students reasoned that different types of fertilizers from nearby residences, animal waste, and dead and decaying organisms would affect the water quality, Le recalls.

Le believes his entomology project could be adapted in schools throughout the United States, wherever science teachers want to help students recognize the relationships among land, air, water, insects, and human activities. "Insects are found everywhere, and the majority of schools in the United States are connected to the Internet, so collaboration among schools on this project is feasible," says Le. "Teachers and students across the country could share their findings, discuss trends, and collaborate on pollution prevention—making their decisions based on sound scientific findings."

Like any worthwhile science project, Entomology on the East Coast requires "careful planning, time, energy, and enthusiasm," reflects Le. "But students end up having such a great appreciation for insects and their role in the ecosystem."

## The Case of the Competing Bakeries

Although state-mandated testing and the perennial problem of limited resources can constrain a science curriculum, the main challenge for many secondary teachers is getting students excited about science.

Dat Le notes that "there are some students who walk into my class on the very first day with a dislike for science. My job is to change that. I have a year to help students to enjoy science again. Through our journey together, hopefully they will have a greater appreciation for science." He adds, "In middle school, students receive fewer experiential, hands-on learning opportunities in the classroom. Often, as students enter middle school, more time in class is devoted to discussions and lectures, which may turn students off. The other reason is students do not see the connection and relevance in science. Teachers need to make that connection to everyday experiences in a child's life."

For one problem-based learning lab that sets up a messy real-life situation, Le's students took on the role of researchers trying to create a fluffier bread for The Yummy Baker, a fictional establishment sadly losing customers to its rival, Light as a Cloud Bakery. Le challenged his students to maximize the amount of carbon dioxide gas in the bread by experimenting with combining different substances, with yeast as a constant. Students connect to this lab, says Le, because "they love to eat" and have some understanding of the variables needed to make yeast produce carbon dioxide.

The open-ended nature of this lab allowed Le's students to choose from a variety of potentially gas-producing reactions or substances, including lemonade, baking soda, vinegar, and various juices and soft drinks. Working in small groups, students created their mixtures in clear plastic bottles, each capped with a balloon, then heated the bottles in a water bath approaching 200 degrees Fahrenheit. Students measured the circumference of the inflating balloons to gauge the relative amount of gas produced in each of several trials. As expected, the range of gas produced in the balloons varied widely; in one case, to students' surprise, the balloon was sucked inside the bottle!

Depending on the needs of each class doing the lab, Le took time to review such terms as *dependent variable* and *independent variable*, and to discuss constants, such as bottle size, amount of yeast, and water bath temperature. He also led a discussion about experimental error and solicited examples from students, who cited incorrect measurements, a loose balloon, or failure to mix the substances. Le also reminded students of the importance of dividing the work among small-group members, both to promote efficiency and to give everyone experience doing the labs.

During a post-lab discussion, students shared their results and together developed a table listing the independent variables. Using two Venn diagrams, the class analyzed the substances that all successful trials had in common, as well as the common ingredients that had produced very little gas. "Students discussed the need to narrow their independent variables to two to four, instead of five to seven. Many discovered that adding vinegar did not produce as much carbon dioxide," Le recalls, a convenient segue to his next unit on testing for pH.

One of Le's goals for his 7th grade classes is for students to understand experimental design "inside and out." Although the lab included some bumps—for example, an attempt to use dishwashing liquid as an independent variable ("Stick to ingredients that would be considered food," Le reminded this group)—Le concluded from the post-lab discussion that his students had gained an understanding of the necessity of careful lab skills and measurement techniques and the need for controlling the constants in repeated trials. "Each day I come to class thinking, How can I improve on what I taught yesterday—or last year? And what can I do to help these students learn and enjoy science?" Le says.

## Natural Science with Michael Fryda

Westside High School in Omaha, Nebraska, is taking a small stab at fighting the compartmentalization of the sciences that has evolved in U.S. schools, as in science itself, during the last 150 years: it's a class titled Natural Science.

"The name was originally intended to convey [science's] eclectic nature," says teacher Michael Fryda, who notes that Natural Science helps students learn a wide array of standards that span the geosciences, astronomy, physics, and chemistry. "A more specific name may lessen students' ability to understand the subdisciplines they'll learn," says Fryda, who proudly points out that Westside personnel consider the "why" of everything they do at their school, including naming courses.

"Science shouldn't be viewed as a subset of disciplines. Some of the strongest scientific principles that have ever been tested have arisen out of a unification of many smaller tested ideas from the subdisciplines. For example, our understanding of plate tectonics and the fossil record has been important for solidifying our modern conception of Darwinian evolution," explains Fryda. "Too many students see science as a set of disjointed, unrelated topics. I want my students to see science as a system of thought made up of many subsets," he emphasizes.

Natural Science also enables students to fulfill the school's graduation requirement that they become familiar with sciences beyond biology (the other required course), should they not take a physics or chemistry class. The science department encourages students to take Natural Science in 9th or 10th grade to give them the foundation for taking more rigorous sciences in higher grades.

## Hooking Students on Science

Fryda takes his Natural Science students through an extended conceptual exploration that, viewed broadly, begins with Earth and expands out to the study of star life cycles. As a kind of counterpoint, the main physical principles of motion and energy are first studied at the macro, everyday level and then as minute forces at the atomic level.

To hook students on the inquiry-based nature of science and the importance of

---

### An Overview of Natural Science

**1st quarter:** The physical concepts of density and pressure provide unifying threads that can explain the rock cycle, plate tectonics, Earth's interior engine of molten rock, and the creation of weather.

**2nd quarter:** A study of Earth's orbit, reasons for the seasons, and the phases of the moon challenge students' preconceptions about these phenomena. Students also study the different views of gravity as explained by Sir Isaac Newton and Albert Einstein, as well as Johannes Kepler's laws of planetary motion. The solar system is then positioned in an exploration of the stars and the scale of the universe.

**3rd quarter:** Students study Newton's laws of motion and use motion detectors to learn about position, speed, velocity, and acceleration in their everyday lives. They also explore heat energy and examine potential and kinetic energy through roller coaster models.

**4th quarter:** Students explore the chemical universe, first by reviewing the changing notions about atomic structure. Then, through a close look at electrons' role in explaining the bonding potential of atoms, students get a better understanding of the periodic table. Discussions about the nature of matter and investigations involving reactions of substances help solidify student understanding about chemical compounds.

using evidence to make decisions, in an initial activity Westside's Natural Science teachers give students information about a "potentially" deadly chemical. Facts about the compound dihydrogen monoxide are selected in such a way as to spin its characteristics in a positive or negative light. "The intent is to show students that information can be painted in a way that warps reality," Fryda says. Once students gather more information, they discover that the mysterious compound is in fact water. This sets the expectation that "students must question all evidence and overcome personal biases as they search for real answers" in science, Fryda explains.

Fryda strives to make science concepts come alive for students by helping them see connections not only among science disciplines but also between science and their prior knowledge. For example, to demonstrate the link between physics and astronomy and to deepen students' understanding about the continuity of the electromagnetic spectrum, he points out to students that the concepts they learned in middle school about the nature and behavior of light and magnetism help modern astronomers collect data about the stars and planets. "That's a lot different from what they're used to seeing. They think of astronomers as looking through light telescopes and *visually* seeing what's going on out in the cosmos," Fryda says.

When appropriate, Fryda also uses popular culture to explore science. Students recently watched the movie *Contact* to gain a more realistic picture of how astronomers collect data via radio waves. They also examine other issues explored in the movie, such as science's effect on society, portrayed in positive and negative lights by different characters, and the perennial human speculation about the presence of other intelligent life in the universe. The latter topic gives the class "a really good opportunity to review concepts of the speed of light and how large these distances are, and how difficult it would be to contact other civilizations if they were out there," Fryda says.

## Emphasizing Problem Solving

The Natural Science course fosters practical understanding of inquiry in a problem-solving framework. Although teachers present students with the problem and materials, students must decide how to design their own experiments. "We want them to logically identify a way that makes sense—with appropriate controls, with the appropriate variables—for us to test an idea," Fryda says.

For example, to address the common misconception that the seasons result from the Earth moving closer to the sun during summer and farther away during winter, Fryda gives students a globe, a lamp, and liquid crystal aquarium thermometers and asks them to design an experiment that will test the difference between direct and indirect light on the heating of the globe. "We work very hard with students to make sure that they are specific, that they have a logical order to their procedure, and that they have an experimental design that will show the different parts of the globe that are getting direct and indirect light rays," he says.

Before conducting the globe-and-lamp experiment, students investigate the concentration of light from a flashlight held at differing angles to reflect off a sheet of graph paper. Students can quantify the different area of light reflection with the graph paper and also make inferences about the relative concentrations of light energy, Fryda says. "We talk about how the energy coming out of the flashlight isn't changing—just like the energy coming out of the sun is not changing. The only difference is that we're spreading that same amount of energy over a bigger area," he explains.

## Improving Communication

Setting clear expectations for students is an ongoing goal that Fryda is continually refining. For a graduate school project, Fryda surveyed students about his manner of communicating expectations. He wanted to know whether students understood what he was asking of them in science class, and how they thought that affected their learning. He especially wanted to test whether his "list of big ideas," the learning expectations that he presents at the beginning of each unit, actually helped them learn. "These big ideas typically combine rote knowledge with higher-order understandings and applications," Fryda says.

What he found intrigued him: female students in particular reported that the big ideas helped them understand the science expectations more than such tactics as verbal reminders or pre-tests. As to why this holistic approach was preferred by girls, Fryda is uncertain. But he knew what he would do: "After that, I communicated expectations in enough different ways that I could be sure that my expectations were clear to male and female students alike."

Fryda now uses many forms of communicating expectations, such as one-on-one verbal feedback, written feedback, pre-tests, classroom posters, and question strings, to make sure that all his students have a clear understanding of what they ought to be learning. Fryda has a feeling that students' increased understanding of expectations results in improved science achievement, and he looks forward to researching that question further as time permits.

In addition, Fryda has been spending time reviewing how he words assessment questions. "A lot of the reasons why students get answers wrong is not that they don't understand the objective, but they don't understand the way in which a question is asked," Fryda contends. At Westside, science teachers have made a concerted effort to "tone down the vocabulary," a major hurdle that many science teachers must overcome, according to Fryda. Now, science teachers are focusing on clearer wording of the "how, what, why, where, and when" of assessment questions that they administer to students.

## Thinking and Writing with a Critical Eye

In Natural Science, writing and assessments go hand in hand. Westside science teachers include conclusion questions at the end of any formative and summative activities to reveal students' thinking processes. "We require students to show us how they use rote knowledge to formulate ideas about science," Fryda says. "Because the general public often finds it extremely difficult to understand science findings, we encourage our students to respond with personal vocabulary and a clear writing style so that their answers could be understood by anyone." Students learn to use the standards of critical thought framed by critical thinking expert Richard Paul (see "Universal Intellectual Standards," p. 56) so that they can better think about how they write.

Fryda displays these standards and guiding questions on a poster at the front of his classroom so that students can refer to them when

## Universal Intellectual Standards

Critical thinking gurus Richard Paul and Linda Elder suggest that the following intellectual standards be applied to thinking "whenever one is interested in checking the quality of reasoning about a problem, issue, or situation."

**1. Clarity:** Could you explain that point further? Could you express that point in another way? Could you give me an example? Clarity is the "gateway standard," state Elder and Paul.

**2. Accuracy:** Is that really true? How could we check that?

**3. Precision:** Could you give more details? Could you be more specific?

**4. Relevance:** How is that connected to the question? How does that bear on the issue?

**5. Depth:** How does your answer address the complexities in the question? How are you taking into account the problem in the question? Is that dealing with the most significant factors?

**6. Breadth:** Do we need to consider another point of view? Is there another way to look at this question? What would this look like from the point of view of . . . ?

**7. Logic:** Does this really make sense? Does that follow from what you said? How does that follow? Before you implied this, and now you are saying that; how can both be true?

*Source:* Adapted from "Universal Intellectual Standards," by L. Elder and R. Paul, 1996. Copyright © 1996 by the Foundation for Critical Thinking. Available: www.criticalthinking.org/resources/articles/universal-intellectual-standards.shtml

they are planning or writing responses to questions. These standards, Fryda claims, represent an often-overlooked element of scientific literacy in the classroom.

Science teachers tend to especially emphasize the standards of accuracy and precision, notes Fryda: "Science is very much about being specific enough that anyone could repeat the work." To instill these two standards in students, Fryda challenges students to verbally explain how to make a peanut butter sandwich. "If they tell us to 'put the peanut butter on the bread' without first telling us to take the bread out of the package, we'll get messy results," Fryda says. He asks his students to look for similar "holes" after they have written their procedures for an experiment in science class.

### Piecing Together Weather with Jigsaw Reading

Fryda and other Westside science teachers ask students to apply the same standards of critical thinking to their readings, which are taken from textbooks, popular science magazines, trade books, and the Internet. Reading with a critical eye is not always easy when the content is particularly dense and complex, however. Fryda notes, for example, that "weather is one of the most difficult sections to teach because it contains so many variables that interact with one another all at the same time. The big disconnect that students have is that they learn the physical principles of how pressure should change with temperature, and how wind speed should change with pressure, and how individual variables we highlight should interact with each other—but then the problem is that all those simple relationships [studied in the classroom] often don't translate well to the reality of very complex weather."

One effective way to grapple with readings on this and other multifaceted subjects is the jigsaw strategy (see "Jigsaw Activity on Weather").

The cooperative nature of the jigsaw activity avoids the problem of every student doing "a whole bunch of busy book work about every concept," says Fryda. "The jigsaw reading is a way for us to get at the complexity of weather. It lets students put the pieces of the content puzzle together and gives all students the opportunity to build literacy skills together. Everybody has the opportunity to be a leader and to be a teacher of someone else."

To ensure that students will teach one another accurately, teachers initially arrange small groups according to ability and then walk around the class to monitor student discussion and notes. A teacher's clarifying questions can get a student on the right path, says Fryda, who notes that direct instruction is used "only as a last resort."

> ## *Jigsaw Activity on Weather*
>
> 1. Students are assigned to home groups. Each member of a given group will become an "expert" on a different topic of weather. These topics include
>
> - Wind and how it's created.
> - Temperature changes on Earth resulting from the sun's energy.
> - Weather fronts.
> - Air pressure.
>
> 2. Each student researches his or her assigned topic using textbook and Web resources.
>
> 3. Topic experts get together and use the standards of critical thought to ensure accuracy and to hone their findings into big ideas.
>
> 4. Students return to their home groups and teach their topics to their groupmates.

## Presenting Data

Data presentation is another important science skill, Fryda tells his students. Although Natural Science is not a math-intensive course, students need math skills to interpret data trends and present high-quality graphs. "We spend a lot of time talking about the nature of presentation and the nature of scale and how it relates to what students want to show. We want to make it clear to students that when they're creating a graph, they're trying to show off their data. A lot of communication in science is making something that will be easy for people to read and understand," Fryda says. Because Natural Science is a graduation requirement for students who may not have had algebra, graphs are fairly simple, usually having two variables.

Organizing data with communication in mind improves students' logic and critical thinking skills because they have to make sense of the data themselves. In addition, students' ability to communicate science knowledge—to convey how they have raised questions and attempted to answer them—is an important part of the inquiry process that has wide applications.

"What I want students to walk away with when they go out into the real world is that science is a discipline of thought, but one that is so closely related to basic problem solving that they can use it in their everyday life—regardless of what their career is," Fryda affirms.

## Chemistry and Physical Science with Paula Young

Science teacher Paula Young thinks the recent increase in chemistry students at Francis Howell North High School in St. Charles, Missouri, is due in part to the opening of a nearby bridge over the Missouri River that has increased access to the school. "We also attribute the increase to *CSI*—the TV show," says Young with a chuckle. Yet she is perfectly serious.

As is her high school—about meeting state expectations for what students should have learned in science by the time they leave high school. Francis Howell North has chosen to require chemistry as a third-year science course, after physical science in 9th grade and biology in 10th grade. Although the district is leaving open the option to tailor chemistry to a conceptually based consumer course or to offer earth science as an alternative, the message is clear: students must take more science.

## Beyond Blah, Blah, Blah

Francis Howell North's increase in science students certainly ups the ante for teachers, who must ensure that each student is engaged with the learning. When Young, who currently teaches chemistry to students in grades 10–12, considers what science lectures might look like in the eyes of students, she's reminded of the *Peanuts* cartoons in which the teacher's talking "comes through as 'blah, blah, blah.'" So Young, a National Science Foundation Presidential Award winner, avoids lecturing as much as possible.

Instead, she prefers to introduce a topic through an exploration activity. A typical lesson sequence goes like this: initial exploration; further concept development through labs; class discussion; library research; student presentations, projects, or "whiteboarding"; and further applications, which might bring students back to more labs, says Young. Using labs as introductory activities "levels the playing field among the students as to their past experience and motivates them to want to know more about the topic," she says.

For example, Young's "dirty water lab" introduces the topic of solutions in chemistry through an inquiry-based lab. To start the lab, students are given a solution of various substances, such as coffee grounds, salt, garlic, and oil, mixed with water. Young challenges pairs of students to "get the water as clean as possible" using knowledge they have already acquired about how water in nature is purified as it percolates through the soil.

Students use such items as charcoal, paper filters, sand, and gravel— alone or in combination—to clean the water. They hypothesize about the effect that each item will have on purifying the water. There is no set procedure, although an earlier textbook version of the activity was more of a cookbook lab, according to Young. Large and small particles are captured by various filtration methods. Students marvel at the properties of activated charcoal, which removes the garlic odor and makes the water "remarkably clean"—although no one wants to drink it, Young jokes. And when the students test the solution for electrical conductivity, the lit bulb shows that dissolved salt remains.

"This leads into a good discussion about particle size and what can be removed by filtration and the separation of materials," Young says. "It's sometimes difficult in chemistry—you don't want to turn students loose with dangerous chemicals in case they design a procedure that could harm them. This is one lab where the chemicals are safe enough that you can turn them loose with them," Young says.

In addition to their role in laying the groundwork for understanding the physical aspects of a concept, labs at Francis Howell North are used to apply concepts learned in culminating projects. In physical science, for example, students are assigned to design a roller coaster to demonstrate their understanding of kinetics. Teams of students including both "engineers" and "advertisers" start by reviewing Web sites about amusement parks and roller coasters to gather ideas for designing their coasters, keeping in mind Newton's dictums and, for their advertising brochures, safety issues.

During the construction phase, students use troughs made of polyurethane pipe insulation cut in half as roller coaster tracks and large steel ball bearings as cars. The goal is to have the ball bearings cycle through the coaster without falling off. Although a team may achieve this on a first run, students typically need to make adjustments to ensure that the bearings safely make their way through the various loops, spirals, and turns of the roller coaster.

## Conveying the Nature of Science

Getting students to understand science means getting them to see that science is a human endeavor that involves a gradual accumulation of contributions from scientists and their experiments and ideas over time. Young herself admires scientists like Einstein or Newton, who took "all of the puzzle pieces" and put them together in one big idea. Young tells students that "these individuals have vision and the ability to see the 'big picture'—it may result from being in the right place at the right time, or from their own genius."

To get a feel for how science concepts are developed and refined over time, students explore a phenomenon for which each of them contributes one piece of knowledge resulting from his or her own experiment.

Students address an urban legend of relatively recent vintage: What happens when you mix Mentos candy with diet soda—and why?

The mixture produces an explosive fountain, and each student researches a different aspect of it: Does the temperature affect the fountain? Does the reaction happen with regular soda? Does it happen with carbonated water? With fruit-flavored instead of mint-flavored Mentos? What does the candy look like under a microscope? One student even adds aspartame to see whether it would make the fountain go higher.

After completing the experiments—outside, of course—students compare their results with those reported on the popular cable TV show *Mythbusters*, which aims to scientifically debunk widespread popular myths, such as whether a penny dropped from a skyscraper could actually kill a person. (No, as it turns out.)

"This later led to a great discussion about atomic structure—how each of us had researched a piece of the Mentos puzzle just like the various scientists had each researched a piece of the puzzle on atomic structure to create a more complete understanding of it," Young says.

Helping students recognize the science behind urban myths and fads and design their own experiments is a fun way to engage all students with the concepts of science. Because Young has students who take chemistry only to get into college and others who enjoy chemistry and plan to pursue college science, she must plan learning activities that take into consideration her students' varying math abilities. "I have to plan activities that are motivating to both the potential chemists and the potential interior designers," she acknowledges.

## The Value of Models

Modeling with manipulatives is another way to meet the needs of a variety of students. In an activity to teach balancing chemical equations, Young has students use small, colorful plastic balls to create three-dimensional models of the equations. She starts by giving students six equations and has them illustrate the arrangements of atoms before and after the reaction by connecting balls using glue sticks or glue guns. Despite the glue, the structures easily come apart for reconfiguration.

"They were able to observe that you must have the same number and kind of elements before and after a reaction—that the elements are just rearranged," Young says. "On later worksheets, I discovered that some students were still drawing pictures of the balls to visualize the reaction." Other students were content to glue balls for a couple of reactions but balanced the rest of the equations by inspection. "This activity gave the students options. I was pleased that some students responded well to the spheres and commented favorably on them," Young says.

Young gives students further opportunities to learn the content by having them work in small groups for peer collaboration; complete practice problems on the whiteboard to provide immediate feedback to Young; and take part in tutoring—online, with Young, or with a peer. Giving students time in class to get started on an assignment also allows students to get extra help right away, she says.

To explain a new concept, Young offers entry points that link with students' prior knowledge. For instance, when learning about the percent composition of compounds, Young first asks students how they typically calculate their percentage of correct answers on a test. Then, in the introductory lab, students calculate the amount of sugar found in a piece of chewing gum as a simple way to grasp the concept of percent composition. Students chew for only five minutes before the sugar is dissolved from this mixture, and the weighing of the gum mass before and after it's chewed yields the mass of the sugar—usually a whopping 60 percent of the total, students find out.

Giving students the opportunity to experience and understand everyday physical phenomena on apparent and atomic levels gives them the groundwork they need to be scientifically literate—one of the main goals of *National Science Education Standards* (NRC, 1996, p. 13).

## Garage Sale Science

Young conducts a workshop on garage sale science for the benefit of her fellow science teachers. "I have the most amazing collection of bowling balls you've ever seen! They are wonderful for physical science—for motion labs on velocity, acceleration, and momentum," Young laughs.

During "inertia ball," a physics activity developed by a colleague, students sweep a bowling ball across the room with a broom. With sets of bowling balls and brooms, Young sets up relay teams of students who must sweep the ball a predetermined distance, while the other teams sweep it back. Students gain a better understanding of Newton's first law of motion, that an object at rest remains at rest unless acted on by an unbalanced force. "The ball is quite massive compared with the straw in the broom, so it requires a bit of effort to place the ball in motion," Young says. As students overcome the bowling ball's inertia, they quickly grasp its relationship to mass, she explains.

Young finds many other uses for garage sale finds as well. At one sale, Young snapped up a box of Styrofoam balls, counting her good fortune and the possibilities of getting her students to create models of crystal structures and various atomic arrangements. For physical science, Young arranges the numerous toys she has picked up at various classroom stations so that students can experience the transfer of spring energy of windup toys, the projectile motion of toy guns that shoot dart-like objects that stick to the walls, a random-motion toy called a Bumble Ball, and yo-yos for circular motion. "There are all kinds of things you can use yo-yos for—they make great pendulums," Young advises. Toys can also be useful in lessons on simple machines, she adds.

It's not only low-tech items that Young finds at garage sales. In her classroom, she has an intranet of five computers purchased at bargain basement prices. Students use these computers to download data from various probe devices that can test temperature, conductivity, pH, and motion.

## Improving Science Communication

In one of Young's favorite lessons, she remains largely in the background. During this lesson, students make presentations on gas laws (which explain the behavior of gases under different conditions) and engage in a modified Socratic dialogue. "It's a successful way to uncover misconceptions and gratifying to observe various students' 'aha!' moments," Young says.

During the presentations, students write down three types of questions to serve as starting points for the dialogue:

**1. A knowledge-based question** (e.g., Will you clarify this content?)

**2. A concept-level or "wondering" question** (e.g., What would happen if . . . ? Why did this happen?)

**3. A broad application question** (e.g., How does the topic of gas laws apply to the community and the world?)

To keep the discussion moving quickly but focused on whomever is speaking, students pass around the "Power Ball," a colorful soccer ball (picked up at a garage sale, of course) that gives the temporary possessor the floor. "This prevents students from blurting out comments or interrupting the speaker," says Young, who notes that male students in particular seem to express their thoughts more carefully than usual when they have the Power Ball in hand. "In that sense, it's a motivating device."

Such student-led discussion provides some major "aha!" moments as students relate the science concepts to their own lives, Young says. For example, when one student talked about cracks appearing in her family's driveway, another better understood the nature of thermal expansion. Students were able to form an analogy between thermal expansion of solids and gases.

Young's involvement in such discussion is minimal; she just enjoys watching students share their science ideas and insights on the topic.

## A Range for Applying Science Technology

Young saw a broad disparity in technology use among science classrooms during her two-year stint as a science technology specialist for urban, suburban, and rural schools throughout Missouri. For example, one rural school had practically no science equipment, so Young visited a local discount store and made a huge list of items—with prices—that could be used in a science lab. "School leaders didn't know you could buy so much science equipment at Wal-Mart!" Young says. One big-ticket item was a microwave oven that could be used to heat water, she recalls. "That school's lack of equipment was the low-tech end of the spectrum."

Interestingly, the computer-based lab probes and accompanying lessons that Young demonstrated during summer professional development workshops did not get as high a rating from teachers as did Young's low-tech labs, such as a lab on conservation of mass that used "Alka-Seltzer, bottles, and balances." Young notes that "teachers wanted things that they could use in their classroom right away and were not as interested in the technology, which surprised me. Schools are at all different stages of technology implementation."

At the high end are probes that can be hooked up to handheld computers or personal digital assistants (PDAs) for data collection. "Their value is they are so motivating to students," Young emphasizes. She adds that for classrooms without computers, PDAs can be a less expensive alternative. Young's students use a class intranet of five computers to crunch data on temperature, conductivity, and pH gathered from probes. In addition, the school's computer labs enable students to conduct Web research, work with science WebQuests, and review with drill-and-practice activities. Young's own Web site allows her to post assignments and helpful links, she says.

Young's SMART Board, an interactive whiteboard that she links to her computer, allows her to share Web simulations, video clips, review games, and PowerPoint presentations with students. When she teaches honors physical science, she shows a simulation for displacement, often a difficult concept for students to grasp. An Internet simulation could show a moving dot zigzagging from its starting point to its resting point, and another moving in a straight line. Both dots have the same displacement, but the simulation shows students the difference between the concepts of distance and displacement, Young explains.

The use of technology not only motivates students, according to Young, but also "most closely approaches what students will be using in college science classrooms or in the 'real world.'" Students who become chemists, for example, will be using computer instruments more than wet labs, Young says. Good technology, in the form of a simulation, can also deepen students' grasp of the science content or even a process skill.

For example, to teach the process of acid-base titration, which makes use of the neutralization between acids and bases to determine the unknown concentration of one or the other in a solution, Young has her students first do a Web simulation by Jerry Wilkinson (see http://science .csustan.edu/chem/titrate/titrate1b.swf). After the simulation, students "seem to do a much better job of hitting the end point [i.e., recognizing the neutralization point], especially if they've never experienced it before," Young says. "The simulation does improve their lab skills."

## Physics with Sam Wheeler

High school teacher Sam Wheeler, who teaches physics at Franklin Academy in Wake Forest, North Carolina, believes that giving students opportunities for lab work is key in getting them to learn that science is a specific way of understanding the world around them. Although facing new challenges at a new school with fewer resources for lab work, Wheeler, a National Science Foundation Presidential Award winner, still calls himself a "big believer in lab and group work." But "mixing it up" to provide a variety of entry points for science knowledge is also important, he adds: "I try to do a combination of labs, discussion, student presentations, lecture, demonstrations, and independent work—when it includes all of that, students don't have time to get their attention going elsewhere."

### Fun with Projectile Motion

In his physics class, Wheeler takes advantage of the many opportunities for hands-on labs and demonstrations to bring home Newton's laws of motion. In a projectile motion unit, for example, he and his students use an eight-foot-long cannon made of PVC piping to launch potatoes across the length of the school soccer field. It's a safe lab, says Wheeler, noting that the combustion, created with aerosol spray and a grill igniter, is contained in the cannon's chamber and that students wear safety goggles.

To deepen their understanding of projectile motion, students calculate various aspects of their shooting spuds. They use measurements of the distance traveled and the cannon's angle to figure out *muzzle velocity*—the speed at which the potato leaves the cannon. Once they know the initial speed of the potato, students can figure out the highest point of its trajectory. Overall, the potato launch provides a clear illustration of two-dimensional motion with projectiles: students understand that the horizontal acceleration remains constant but that vertical acceleration toward the ground increases because of gravity, explains Wheeler.

Back in the classroom lab, groups of students use similar calculations to predict the precise trajectory of a marble shoot. With the help of a launcher crafted from Hot Wheels tracks, a ring stand, and duct tape, a marble typically travels a meter's length into a waiting cup. "They have to demonstrate their prediction in front of me, and I only give them one shot to get it right!" says Wheeler, who jokes with his students that marbles that miss get teams an "automatic *F*."

Before their launch, teams show Wheeler their calculations, which he checks for accuracy to give them a last chance to revise faulty work. "They have to understand the concept of projectile motion in detail, or their experiment doesn't work," emphasizes Wheeler. "The expectations, the 'false stress' of the evaluation, and the fun of the lab make this lesson work."

## Far-Flung, Hands-On Professional Development

"The more you know, or the more experienced you are with the topic, the more excitement you can bring to the class," advises Wheeler, who is constantly on the lookout for unusual professional development opportunities. Wheeler prefers programs that allow him to work as a field scientist so that he can bring back that experience to his students. For example, one summer he went to Alberta, Canada's Dinosaur Provincial Park on an archaeological dig for dinosaur bones. Wheeler ended up excavating bones from a duck-billed herbivore called a hadrosaur.

"It's a 'veggiesaurus'—we didn't find any tyrannosauruses, but it was still pretty cool!" he recalls. "There are so many bones up there that you can see them exposed on the ground." So many, in fact, that the park's Royal Tyrrell Museum has nowhere to put them, he adds.

Wheeler's participation in the dinosaur dig (and in other professional development institutes in Ecuador, Belize, and Yellowstone National Park) was sponsored through the North Carolina Museum of Natural Sciences' Educators of Excellence program. Upon their return from such experiences, participating teachers must develop a related lesson plan to share their knowledge with their students. After the dig in Canada, Wheeler created a lesson for his AP physics class that helped students understand the relationship between the depth of a dinosaur fossil footprint and the dinosaur's estimated weight.

"Since these creatures walked on mud or sand, they'll make a footprint that will have a certain depression caused by weight," Wheeler points out. He devised a way to measure the depth of the footprint and estimate the weight of the dinosaur by using a *bulk modulus*. The bulk modulus formula yields the change in volume of a solid substance based on the pressure exerted on it, so Wheeler used it to quantify a relationship between the force behind a footprint and its depth.

For the lab, he gave students a bucket of dirt to determine how much the dirt would compress under different weights. After calibrating those weights, students took turns stepping into the dirt to get a rough estimate of their own weight based on the depth of their footprints. "It's not exact, but close enough for the student level, so they could see that relationship," says Wheeler. He hopes that he can further develop the lab to have students estimate the mass of a dinosaur using casts of fossil footprints.

Lab lessons like those used by Wheeler and the other seasoned science teachers constitute the most significant and engaging way to provide students with the practical inquiry skills of science. Lab work does present its own challenges in terms of time management, acquisition of resources, and integration of labs with content, as the National Research Council's *America's Lab Report: Investigations in High School Science* concludes (see "The Status of the Science Lab"). In the coming years, educators should expect further efforts from the science education research community to find the best ways of using science labs to enhance student understanding.

# The Status of the Science Lab

*Deborah Perkins-Gough*

Laboratory investigations have been part of the science curriculum in U.S. high schools for two centuries. Unfortunately, the quality of these laboratory experiences is poor for most students, according to *America's Lab Report: Investigations in High School Science*, published by the National Research Council (NRC). To produce this report, an NRC-appointed committee of experts reviewed the research and held a series of public fact-finding meetings exploring the history, current status, and future of science laboratory classes in the United States. The committee's conclusion: laboratory experiences need to change to support meaningful learning about both the scientific process and important science concepts.

## Purposes of Science Laboratory Experiences

The committee found that there is no consensus among policy-makers, educators, and researchers about the purposes—or even the basic definition—of laboratory experiences. The committee concluded that science education must include opportunities for students to learn about both the process and the content of science. Laboratory experiences should teach students about scientific processes by enabling students "to interact directly with the material world (or with data drawn from the material world), using the tools, data-collection techniques, models, and theories of science." Specific learning goals for lab experiences include

- Enhancing mastery of subject matter.
- Developing scientific reasoning.
- Understanding the complexity and ambiguity of empirical work.
- Developing practical skills.
- Understanding the nature of science.

- Cultivating interest in science and in learning science.
- Developing teamwork abilities.

**Today's Laboratory Classes**

No single lab experience is likely to achieve all of these goals, and the report notes that high school science classes should, and do, use a wide variety of approaches. Many laboratory classes require that students follow specified procedures to verify established scientific knowledge. Others engage students in developing questions, designing investigations, and generating explanations.

The major flaw in today's typical high school lab experiences, notes the report, is their lack of connection with the flow of classroom science lessons. Science teachers and laboratory manuals often emphasize procedures instead of setting out clear learning goals, leaving students uncertain about what knowledge and understandings they are supposed to gain. The laboratory experience rarely incorporates ongoing reflection and discussion among the teacher and students about science concepts connected to the activities. In addition, most high school students participate in a limited range of lab activities. Additional findings include the following:

- The average high school student takes three years of science courses before graduation and participates in one laboratory class period each week.
- The amount of time students spend in laboratory courses varies according to ethnicity.
- Students in schools with high proportions of non-Asian minorities tend to spend less time in lab-related activities than do schools with lower proportions of minorities.

Why are traditional laboratory experiences still so prevalent in U.S. high schools? The report cites a number of factors working against change. Foremost is teacher preparation: undergraduate teacher education programs rarely prepare future teachers with the pedagogical and science content knowledge they need to integrate student learning of science processes and important science content. Professional development opportunities for science teachers are limited and usually place little emphasis on laboratory instruction. School laboratory facilities and supplies are often inadequate, particularly in schools serving low-income and minority communities. Finally, rigid school schedules and state science standards that mandate teaching extensive lists of science topics in a given grade may discourage teachers from adopting more effective approaches to laboratory instruction, which often require extended time for discussion and reflection.

## What Science Labs Should Look Like

The last 10 years have seen a trend toward more integrated instructional units that connect lab experiences with other science learning activities, such as lectures, reading, and discussion. On the basis of emerging research on such units, the report concludes that effective laboratory experiences

- Are designed with clear learning outcomes in mind.
- Are thoughtfully sequenced into the flow of classroom instruction.
- Are designed to integrate learning of science content with learning about the processes of science.
- Incorporate ongoing student reflection and discussion.

Because integrated science curriculums are relatively rare, the research evidence is insufficient to support detailed recommendations about specific policies or programs. The report concludes that "a serious research agenda is required to build knowledge of how various types of laboratory experiences (within the context of science education) may contribute to specific science learning outcomes."

*America's Lab Report: Investigations in High School Science* (2005) is available from The National Academies Press at www.nap.edu/catalog/11311.html.

*Source:* Adapted from "Special Report: The Status of the Science Lab," by D. Perkins-Gough, 2006, *Educational Leadership, 64*(4), pp. 93–94. Copyright © 2006 by Association for Supervision and Curriculum Development.

## Reflections  ◆  ◆  ◆

Bringing the science curriculum to life in the classroom relies largely on the teacher's content knowledge, confidence, and creative thinking. Yet a well-planned curriculum that effectively marries the content of science with the lab work and hands-on experiences so crucial for fostering scientific inquiry skills and conceptual understanding can have a strong positive influence on student learning when taught with fidelity, say experts. One trait stands out among the science teachers featured in this chapter: their desire to keep learning about their craft, whether through self-reflection, collegial learning communities, or formal programs of professional development.

# Fresh Approaches to Teaching Urban and Minority Students

# 4

*I do feel, in my dreamings and yearnings, so undiscovered by those who are able to help me.*

—*Mary McLeod Bethune*

U.S. urban schools have the highest concentration of minority students in the country. They also produce bleak statistics for student performance on science assessments. Researchers and urban educators are striving to improve the situation by trying out new approaches to engage students in the culture of science. Nonetheless, it's an uphill battle for typical urban school districts fraught with complex problems involving poverty, lack of resources, and substandard teaching and school organization.

The 2006 National Assessment of Educational Progress (NAEP), a nationwide test that compares student achievement across state and district lines, reported that students in 10 urban school districts earned lower average scores in science than did their public school peers in the rest of the United States. The assessments covered topics in biology, chemistry, earth science, and physics (Lutkus, Lauko, & Brockway, 2006). Average science scores for 4th and 8th grade students in 9 of the 10 districts—Atlanta, Boston, Charlotte (North Carolina), Chicago, Cleveland, Houston, Los Angeles, New York, and San Diego—fell below the national average at both grade levels. Fourth graders in the 10th district—Austin, Texas—performed at the national average, but the district's 8th graders fell below their peers nationwide.

To put those comparisons in context, consider the overall mediocre state of U.S. science education according to the 2006 NAEP:

• Only 29 percent of U.S. 4th and 8th graders garnered a "proficient" rating in science.

• Only 18 percent of 12th graders were considered proficient, and that grade level's average 2005 scores were significantly lower than the 1996 scores.

• About 34 percent of 4th graders and 43 percent of 8th graders ranked in the lowest category, "below basic." At 8th grade, this means that students were unable to carry out investigations or interpret data and graphs.

• About 46 percent of 12th graders ranked in the below basic category. These students were unable to design steps for an investigation or show an understanding of scientific models, systems, or patterns of change.

## Ambivalent Attitudes Toward Science

Evidence shows that many urban minority students are well aware of the importance of science and the deficiencies of their school programs. A recent survey shows that black students, more than white or Latino students, believe that not being taught enough math and science is a "serious problem" that can affect their success in the outside world (Johnson, Arumi, Ott, & Remaley, 2006). The same survey also notes that black students are more likely than white students to say that increasing math and science courses would improve their high school education.

In their research synthesis *Science Education and Student Diversity* (2006), Okhee Lee and Aurolyn Luykx point to studies that show the many gaps between the aspirations of minority students in science and the means they have for fulfilling them.

One study of black middle school students showed that although they were achievement oriented and even aspired to science-related careers, they were ambivalent about science class and about pursuing science at the high school level (Lee & Luykx, 2006). Another study revealed that minority students had a positive attitude toward science and considered pursuing science careers but that their science grades, inquiry skills, and access to knowledge that would help them realize that goal were limited compared with those of white students (Lee & Luykx, 2006).

## Cultural Disconnects

Some science and diversity researchers see modern Western science as the dominant cultural mode with which students from marginalized groups may not resonate for a variety of complex reasons. To have such students understand and succeed in science, teachers need to make the norms of science even more explicit.

Through modeling and by taking an initially directive approach that "unpacks" the nature of science, teachers can help students "who come from backgrounds in which questioning and inquiry are not encouraged" to learn to explore, take the initiative, and assume the responsibility for their own learning (Lee & Luykx, 2006). Although this has to be done for all students—even those in white, affluent, suburban schools—the research shows that bridging such cultural gaps with nonmainstream groups can be more problematic.

For example, Okhee Lee's work with Haitian immigrants in Miami shows that students who speak English at school and Haitian Creole at home must also negotiate between two different sets of cultural expectations about school instruction. The dissonance can sometimes interfere with teachers' perceptions of students' science performance and, conversely, with students' and parents' understandings of what ought to be happening in the classroom.

According to Lee, the Haitian American community—formed by the highly didactic, teacher-centered school system in Haiti—demonstrates a "unanimous response" about how students should behave at school: respect the teachers, don't talk back, be quiet, do what teachers tell you, and recite back. Haitians tend to see U.S. schools as unruly and undisciplined, with lots of students talking back to teachers, Lee says, noting that "they are proud of the Haitian school system." Lee adds, "So when kids come to science, and teachers ask, 'Do you have any questions?'—students don't have questions. Teachers think students don't care, that they are not participating, or that they don't understand. The kids think they are doing OK—but then are told the opposite."

Lee points out research showing that students from diverse backgrounds "deploy sense-making practices—deep questions, vigorous argumentation, situated guesswork, embedded imagining, multiple perspectives, and innovative uses of everyday words to construct new meanings—that serve as intellectual resources in science learning" (Lee & Luykx, 2006, p. 47). Research shows that Haitian children, quiet and respectful in the classroom, will, in a "culturally familiar environment," hold animated arguments about science "in a way that is integral to Haitian culture" and that meshes with scientific practice, Lee states.

To bridge cultural and language gaps and build understanding in science, a good teacher will ask students from other countries, cultures, or language groups about their science background, "then she will observe the students, try to accommodate them, and make them more comfortable," Lee says. At the same time, even as the teacher encourages students to use open ways of questioning and addressing the teacher in the classroom, she should also remind students that such methods may not be appropriate at home with parents or other adults in their families.

"If teachers have an understanding of the norms and practices of science, teachers will be able to make bridges that the students need," Lee says. Building relationships with students who have come from marginalized groups provides that "safe environment" that encourages such students to take part in learning science: "A good teacher is sensitive to both the academic and the emotional needs of students."

## A Two-Way Street to Success

When science education researcher Kenneth Tobin taught in a crowded inner-city Philadelphia high school whose population consisted mostly of African American students living in conditions of poverty, he quickly recognized that his previous experiences teaching science in sedate middle-class settings did little to help him reach students. Tobin was faced with many students who slept in class, talked out of turn, defied his authority, and refused to engage in his science lessons.

Tobin initially scrambled to build relationships with students and increase their interest in science by focusing on those who wanted to learn, providing choice, promoting hands-on science, and getting support from students' families. But he soon realized that the disconnect between most of his students and science was not something that would be mended quickly.

Since his experience teaching chemistry and physics in Philadelphia, Tobin, now an education professor at the City University of New York, has developed further strategies to address the problems that beset urban science education. With National Science Foundation funding, Tobin and his colleagues have worked in New York City public schools to find better ways to teach science to urban students and to train new science teachers. Their various approaches, rooted in the school of critical ethnography that seeks to expose inequities and find practical solutions to address them, are outlined in detail in *Improving Urban Science Education: New Roles for Teachers, Students, and Researchers* (Tobin, Elmesky, & Seiler, 2005).

"When you're dealing with kids who come from conditions of poverty, and kids with an urban youth culture that they bring to the table, it gets denied by the school. It's very difficult for teachers who usually are from some other ethnic background. You have teachers having to learn new cultures, and kids having to learn a new culture in order to make classrooms click," Tobin explains. In contrast, he notes, middle-class or suburban schools can have more homogeneous settings—the cultures that kids bring from home fit in more with the cultures that teachers bring from home.

Much of Tobin's work focuses on building cultural and emotional bridges in the classroom through a process called *cogenerative dialogue*. In essence, it's conversation between the teacher and the students about shared experiences in the classroom. "The idea is to get kids, who are diverse, in the classroom to sit and talk with their teacher or teachers about what's happening, and to talk about the shared experience, and to figure out ways to improve the classroom, whether by changing the roles, the rules, or the resources that are available to students," Tobin explains. "When kids get involved in cogenerative dialogues, we find that enormous changes take place. Classrooms become less corporate and more communal. The emotions in the classroom become very positive."

Authentic collaboration with students is part of a strategy to "maximize positive emotional energy and minimize negative emotional energy," Tobin says. Raising the ante on minor infractions often turns into useless power struggles that result in humiliation for either the student or the teacher. While quite demoralizing for teachers, such dynamics also turn off students, who just "check out" by sleeping, chatting, causing disruptions, or skipping class entirely.

"If teachers engage in cogenerative dialogues, kids are able to change their practices and the way they engage and a lot of the rules that allow them to participate in class. They do better on those tests. They turn up to school. There are fewer discipline problems. They talk to teachers rather than just go through the motions. Getting more student buy-in leads to better performance on high-stakes tests—it's not the major focus of our work, but we have some evidence of that," Tobin acknowledges.

The process is not easy, says Tobin, and requires that teachers rethink their own practices. In one Brooklyn "discipline school," students asked that they be allowed to sit in science labs together with members from their street gangs or neighborhoods. The changes arising from such discussions often go against conventional teacher wisdom. In this case, however, as a result of the student buy-in to the common enterprise of science, cooperation increased across gangs as well as cultures, Tobin notes.

Although students need to learn the terms of "canonical science," allowing them to express their understanding in their own lingo also keeps open positive lines of communication. For example, during one discussion, a student compared the movement of nerve impulses across synapses to the transportation system that brings people to his gritty urban neighborhood's "Dirty Block," where drug selling, prostitution, and other illicit activities occur (Seiler, 2002).

In another case, students brought in their favorite basketball video games and related the concepts of momentum, acceleration, and force to the action of the digital players on the screen. "Whether the physics is really good or not is quite another matter. But [the video] is a gateway to talking about these terms and coming to understand them," Tobin points out. He adds, "You can't have a situation where schools deny what kids do and know. The curriculum has to be built around what kids bring to the table. It lets them connect the science to what they do every day and what they find to be relevant and important. It opens the doorway to learning."

## Cogens in Action

Christopher Emdin, himself a Bronx native, recently taught physics and chemistry at the Bronx's Marie Curie High School for Nursing, Medicine, and Allied Health Professions. Based on the small specialized school model, Marie Curie opened in 2004 to prepare students in grades 7–12 for college studies in the health professions with a rigorous program in math, science, and interdisciplinary studies. Its population of 400-plus students is a mixture of African American and Latino students.

Emdin, who while teaching also became a researcher and doctoral candidate under Tobin at the City University of New York, regularly schedules lunch-time cogenerative dialogues, called "cogens" for short, with small groups of students. Emdin's cogens typically take on the following format:

1. **Videotape the class lesson.** The video provides the material for students and teacher to discuss.

2. **Invite four to five students to participate in the cogenerative dialogue.** Emdin asks for volunteers but seeks to represent the entire class. In his physics class, students tend to sort themselves by ethnicity or culture—African American, Mexican, Dominican, and so on—so Emdin makes sure to pick volunteers from each group.

3. **Set ground rules for talking.** Rules include showing mutual respect, not talking over others, and sharing ideas. It may take four to five sessions before students get these rules down, Emdin says.

4. **Play the videotape of the lesson.** Start, pause, rewind, and replay the video as appropriate. Students and teacher share their thoughts, observations, insights, and recommendations.

**5. Formulate the theme of the discussion.** Typically, says Emdin, the conversations develop an overriding theme, which becomes the focal point of the discussion and recommendations.

**6. Remind participants of the goal.** As the session winds down, Emdin reminds students of the cogen's aim—to agree on one thing before they finish that can improve the teaching and learning in their classroom.

One cogenerative dialogue led by Emdin centered on a physics lesson in which he had demonstrated drawing free-body diagrams—a schematic of an object (drawn as a box) with arrows emanating from it to depict the degree and types of forces acting on the object in a given situation. During the cogen, a student started by sharing that she still didn't understand the concept. The rest of her peers joined in agreement. It was a blow to his ego, Emdin recalls: "I thought I had done a great job with that lesson."

So Emdin provided a running commentary on the video of the lesson, explaining to students his intentions and the points he *thought* he had made. Students gained a better understanding of his goals and, now that they understood, told Emdin that they would prefer to draw the diagrams on the board themselves rather than watch him do it.

Revisiting the lesson in class, Emdin had students create their own free-body diagrams in class presentations. He was pleasantly surprised to hear students using science terms—*applied force, force of gravity, coefficient of friction*—in appropriate ways. He attributes their grasp of the terms and overall concept to the cogen. In general, he has found that giving students more control increases their interest in science, noting that "when a suggestion they make in a cogen gets implemented in class," students feel more socially involved, which "has proven to almost always equate to extra effort or interest in the subject."

During another cogen—this one during class and without a videotape—students discussed the fact that they had no out-of-school rituals or routines that supported science learning. So they developed science-related activities to integrate into their daily routines, such as quizzing one another on the bus ride to school. Over time, these new rituals became commonplace in students' everyday lives.

As Emdin reviews class videotapes, he can zero in on teaching practices that generate both learning and positive responses from students. During a physics class discussion about distance versus displacement, Emdin brought up a recent student race around a local reservoir. The contest winner happened to be in the classroom and was proud of his time on the four-mile race.

"I told Carlos, 'Yeah, maybe you won—but you still had zero displacement,'" Emdin recalls. Eyebrows raised, the class noise level went down, and the student clenched his jaw. The exchange could easily have become negative, Emdin admits, especially as the student raised his voice against Emdin's apparent challenge. As a countermeasure, Emdin lowered the register of his own voice to defuse the building tension.

He explains, "I could have read it as negative tension—but I read it as positive" because it heightened student interest in the science. As students thought a bit longer about the difference between displacement and distance—the race was a circuit—"the ahas and smiles came, and the body language eased," he says.

The experience was formative for Emdin's own teaching, he says, because it taught him how to build classroom excitement and hold tension in the balance. "Through that experience, I learned to let students process the information first."

Another benefit of cogenerative dialogues is the confidence it gives students to share their ideas in class or to teach other, often younger, students what they have learned in science. Emdin has taken part in Tobin's coteaching project, in which student teachers pair up to teach in urban schools (sometimes with a third, experienced teacher), and concludes that "cogens breed coteachers." Students are more willing to share their ideas in class because they are taken seriously. And certain students have become "excellent at creating examples that relate everyday life to physics," Emdin says.

For example, during a discussion on Newton's laws of motion, one student brought up the fact that the train stops so abruptly at the Kingsbridge subway station near the school that passengers often lose their balance and fall over. Students at first talked about the applied force needed to stop the train, but their further questions and insights made them realize that the platform of this subway station was shorter than others on the line. They conjectured that the driver must apply greater force over a shorter distance to align the train so that all the cars can be entered from the platform. "This all came out of cogenerative dialogues," says Emdin.

Beyond science content, cogens also address such issues as New York State's Regents Exams. Talking about the test is different from teaching to the test, Emdin says: "The process of testing or preparing for a test becomes a topic that students discuss rather than an end that they move toward. From day one, they design ways in which they can succeed in the class and on the test. This includes the development of test-taking techniques in addition to discussion of the content."

Even if students use informal street talk to discuss their dissection of a frog, for example, they also acquire the necessary scientific terms and learn to move back and forth between the two languages. "Students' 'hybridized' science knowledge is validated in the classroom but not used to replace canonical understandings," Emdin emphasizes. "Both approaches to science are valued and accepted. Students develop both understandings and furthermore know when and where which type of knowledge is appropriate through discussions about the differences in cogens," he says.

Getting all students to participate in cogens can be a challenge, Emdin admits, and teachers need to take care to prevent any one group from dominating. To encourage all students to engage in the cogens, which take place throughout the entire school year, Emdin asks initial participants to invite their friends from class, and he allows students to opt out after five sessions. The best feeling of all, says Emdin, is when students themselves request a cogen because they believe that a lesson has not gone well or they don't understand the content.

## Designing a Curriculum with Students in Mind

Gale Seiler is a former colleague of Kenneth Tobin's at City High School in Philadelphia. A veteran science teacher in urban settings and now an education professor at McGill University in Montreal, Seiler maintains that recent reforms have failed to improve education—especially the education of inner-city African American students living in poverty (Seiler, 2001). Science education therefore has to change to engage these students in new ways, Seiler contends.

Although she welcomes No Child Left Behind as a means to shed more light on the disparity between the education of urban students and the schooling of their suburban peers, Seiler believes that in many ways the situation has worsened in high-needs, low-performing schools. "The pressure to ensure that students pass state tests has become so great on district- and school-level administrators that they are resorting to science teaching that resembles direct instruction," Seiler observes.

In urban Maryland school districts, for example, schools are using prepackaged curricula that provide full lesson plans linked to state standards, as well as textbook readings, worksheets, assessments, and labs or virtual labs, structured around a minute-by-minute timetable.

"These types of curricula are not inherently bad. They do, however, tend to lead to a type of teaching that relies heavily on recipe-like adherence to the lessons," Seiler notes. Novice teachers, who are common in high-turnover urban schools, often use such plans. In doing so, they avoid "grappling with their own understanding of the content" and miss connections between content and unifying themes of science, Seiler explains.

## Beyond the Science Lunch Group

When she taught at City High School, Seiler created a weekly lunch group for African American males to enable them to share ideas about science in an informal but respectful setting. Like Tobin, Seiler had been shocked not only by the lack of student interest in classes but also by teachers' low expectations of students, the fragmented curriculum, the lack of lab activities, and uninspired teaching methods consisting of lectures and handouts.

Seiler found that when students were encouraged to discuss and analyze investigations during the science group meetings, they brought in appropriate scientific terms, drew useful analogies, and offered alternate ways to approach an investigation to advance their understanding

(Seiler, 2001). These were the students who would typically be labeled "at risk" and deemed incapable of succeeding in college. "From the experience of the lunch group, it becomes apparent how great is the magnitude of the talent and curiosity being squandered and the opportunities being lost by such students being positioned as silent recipients of education," writes Seiler (2001, p. 1010).

Seiler concluded that science teachers in urban schools could take better advantage of their students' personal experiences, which typically go unrecognized, and relate them to science. For example, during one of her group's lunch discussions, about the physics of sound and the various pitches produced by different wavelengths, one student who played drums explained to his peers how tightening keys around the drumhead changes the pitch. Another student, who worked part-time in a barbershop, then noted how the buzzing sound of an electric hair clipper alters in tone when a blade needs tightening. These experiences from students' everyday lives provided relevant and personal connections to science.

To reap further fruit from the science lunch group project, Seiler embedded what she learned directly into the 10th grade curriculum, designed to prepare students for the Pennsylvania System of School Assessment in biology. Seiler sought to "combine planning with responsive flexibility" to give students "choice and voice," she says. The biology curriculum is structured around the following essential elements, the first three of which should be a familiar part of any master teacher's curricular and instructional repertoire:

1. **Science standards:** The curriculum addresses national, state, and district standards for life science content and scientific literacy.

2. **Driving questions:** The curriculum includes high-interest questions that connect students' concerns, cultures, and personal lives with science concepts.

3. **Inquiry groups:** The curriculum has students working cooperatively to raise additional questions and evaluate information that will help answer the driving questions.

4. **Cultural resonance:** The curriculum gives students the chance to make connections to their particular interests, environments, and cultures.

The starting point of the biology curriculum is the NRC's *National Science Education Standards*. Underlying the curriculum are the unifying concepts of "systems, order, and organization" and "evidence, models, and explanation." The curriculum encompasses numerous topics, including the characteristics of living things, structure and function in biological organization, cell structure, mitosis and meiosis, inheritance, molecular genetics, natural selection, and population biology.

Driving questions, generated in part by the students' interests, included "Why is pro basketball player Yao Ming so tall?" and "Why did Alonzo Mourning stop playing basketball?" The first question covers content on genetics and inheritance, whereas the question about Mourning, who had a kidney disease, addresses issues about homeostasis, cellular respiration, and structure-function relationships, among other science concepts.

Because students are highly engaged in these driving questions and are tackling content "on a want-to-know basis," they become more comfortable bringing science vocabulary, concepts, and practices into their "ways of being in class and doing science," according to Seiler.

Seiler contends that most science classes—whether white or black, urban or suburban—only approximate what a community of scientists do: "Most high school students do not do authentic science, but they do school science, and in most schools this is a mixture of school norms, community norms, and a particular approach to science employed by the teacher." Therefore, approaches to school science—while retaining certain essential elements found in all sciences—can be altered in some aspects to engage and motivate different groups of students.

"For severely marginalized students, many of whom are on the verge of dropping out, access to mainstream science is not the issue. Keeping them engaged in something so they will stay in school is the first step. . . . I believe that science has a greater potential for this type of engagement than other subjects, due to its nature built on curiosity and understanding of the world around us. Ironically, it often is the discipline that serves as a gatekeeper instead of the motivator," Seiler points out. Seiler's research in urban schools with predominantly African American student populations has yielded several practices that science teachers can use

# Urban African American Students and Science: Strengthening Connections

*Gale Seiler*

LISTEN TO STUDENTS. Teachers can change the way they "hear" things in their classrooms. Be open to what the students contribute and how they make contributions. Listen to students' analogies, connections, and questions. Students' efforts to connect science to their lives are often shut down by teachers because they are outside traditional science—or perhaps outside white, mainstream norms—in terms of how they are expressed. Through videotaping science classrooms, my research has focused on efforts that students make to contribute and how these efforts are often devalued by the teacher or may even get the students in trouble! Classroom recordings have revealed that much talk perceived as off-task or "off the wall" is not what it appears.

SEE STUDENTS' ACTIONS IN NEW WAYS. For African American students, this means letting students *move* in the classrooms. Learn about your students. Only when teachers *know* their students can they understand them and connect science with their students' lives and create room for students to do the same. This last part is key. I believe that most students will try to make this connection, but it may look different from what we expect it to look like. We can't recognize it for what it is unless we know our students.

PROVIDE STUDENT CHOICE AND VOICE IN GUIDING THE CURRICULUM AND DAY-TO-DAY LESSONS. Build in options and give students some voice. Follow their lead. Yes, you have to equip them with certain understandings, but come on, be creative! There are any number of "right" ways to do that for a given topic. Who says we have to teach the parts of a heart before we have students dissect one? Why does it have to be so linear? Voice and choice take on major dimensions for

African American students, who are frequently devalued by society and schools.

**EXAMINE ASSUMPTIONS ABOUT YOUR STUDENTS.** Urban (and suburban) teachers ought to challenge their worldview and gain a new perspective on their students—see strengths where they only saw deficits. We make quick judgments in the classroom that emanate from our tacit understandings. For many whites, these include a perspective that is shaped by a "smog of racism," as Beverly Daniel Tatum put it. How we respond to students happens in the moment, and unless we have worked hard to remove negative stereotypes from our schema, we respond from that place.

**SEEK EFFECTIVE CHANGES.** Each teacher needs to figure out how he or she can alter the structure of the school and classroom to resonate with their disadvantaged students and motivate them to learn science. Teachers don't all have to do it in the same way, but we do all have to find a way that works for each of us. Realize that it is not going to happen overnight but that structure and agency are recursively related, and change in one creates opportunities for change in the other.

to better understand their inner-city students and help them connect to science (see "Urban African American Students and Science: Strengthening Connections").

## Supporting English Language Learners in Science

*The Condition of Education 2006* (National Center for Education Statistics [NCES], 2006) notes that U.S. schools are the most diverse they have been in history. The report shows that between 1972 and 2004, racial and ethnic minorities increased from 22 to 43 percent of total enrollment in U.S. public schools, with Latino students accounting for nearly half of the total minority enrollment. Nearly one-fifth of children ages 5–17 speak a language other than English at home.

Many English language learners (ELLs) have literacy difficulties that stymie their understanding and enjoyment of science, a vocabulary- and concept-intensive subject if ever there was one. Addressing these literacy needs in tandem with an inquiry-based, hands-on approach to science can help students become more proficient in both science and English.

A proven strategy for engaging students in science is making connections to everyday life through personal interests, community issues, and family ties. One of the most powerful things students can realize is the uniquely human pleasure of learning and problem solving in the field or the lab—what *National Science Education Standards* calls "science as a human endeavor" (NRC, 1996, p. 139).

"One thing we know is that the more education you have, the better off you'll be economically. You'll have a better chance of success in this life. The more science and math you know, again, the better off you'll be economically—and you'll fit in better into this culture or whatever culture is going to be around 20 years from now," says Michael Padilla, past president of the NSTA and science education professor at the University of Georgia.

Unfortunately, students from non-English-speaking families have extra hurdles to jump to get this education. They have to overcome language barriers just to make sense of everyday English, not to mention become proficient at academic reading and writing, Padilla notes.

Like many countries, the United States must accommodate growing cultural and linguistic diversity resulting from immigration. In urban schools, students from other countries may represent a dozen or more cultures or languages. These students are at risk of low achievement or dropping out of school because their generally limited knowledge of English hinders their understanding.

"You realize the difficulty of a kid who comes over here at age 7 or 10 and doesn't understand English. It takes five to six years to get up to snuff to be able to do their academic work in English—and yet they are taught in English," Padilla says. "Then all of a sudden, they're in 8th grade and they are *way* behind, and the likelihood of dropping out is high. It starts this terrible cycle of dropping out because they're not doing well," which, in turn, can contribute to their own children under-achieving, Padilla adds.

## Bridging the Cultural Gap

Padilla believes that parents, students, and educators alike will ben-efit from even small mutual efforts at cross-cultural exchange within the classroom. In 2001–2002, minority students accounted for 4 in 10 students in U.S. public schools. Of these, Latino children make up the largest and fastest-growing group, comprising about 20 percent of K–12 U.S. public school enrollment in 2004 (NCES, 2006). Especially in dis-tricts where immigrant enrollment is growing, administrators and teach-ers unused to language issues must make an extra effort to help students master academic use of English.

In addition, educators should be aware of cultural differences that can hinder academic achievement for ELLs. Padilla points out, for exam-ple, that "Latino families tend to be very supportive but hands-off about their children's education. That doesn't fit well with the U.S. system." In other words, Latino parents may not realize that they, rather than the teacher, may be the key to getting their children to study. "A kid might go home and say, 'No homework,'" says Padilla, but Latino parents—like any parents—need to follow up. Schools should foster an understand-ing about how the school system works at both the classroom and the administrative level to help parents monitor their children better and to give them the know-how to push for their children's interests in the school or district.

Padilla cautions that building cultural knowledge shouldn't be a one-way street; teachers and administrators should make the effort to learn about the workings of immigrants' native school systems and societies. In Georgia, 75 percent of Latino students come from Mexico, he says, so if a teacher can understand transcripts from Mexican schools, he or she will have a better idea of what students have already learned. Bridging that communication gap at the cultural and administrative levels will help teachers focus on students as individuals, Padilla explains.

## Promoting Science Literacy and Understanding

Learning the complex concepts of science, complete with their specialized vocabulary, is always challenging—but even more so for English language learners. Padilla suggests helping Latino students learn science vocabulary by drawing parallels with cognates from Spanish. For example, words such as *insect, magnification,* and *machine* have the Spanish cognates of *insecto, magnificación,* and *máquina.* If scientific terms are new to all language groups in the class, however, some experts advise introducing and reinforcing these terms in English. *Science for English Language Learners: K–12 Classroom Strategies* suggests ways to partner language arts with science to mutual advantage, including "representing" a text for deeper understanding through role playing, cooperative dialogue, and genre-transforming exercises (Maatta, Dobb, & Ostlund, 2006, p. 41):

• **Role playing.** Students act out the text that they have read. For example, students could take on the roles of organisms in the food chain, from plankton to humans, and act out the series of who eats whom.

• **Cooperative dialogue.** Teams of students write a dialogue based on a text. For example, after reading about erosion in a unit on landforms, students could write a discussion that home builders might have before starting construction on a hill or beachfront.

• **Genre-transforming exercises.** Students rewrite a text into another genre. For example, students could turn a passage about the growth cycle of a plant into a storyboard with pictures and simple captions.

Adapting text and modifying language can also help students focus on important terms and concepts. "I think it can be overwhelming to see all of the text material and handout material in biology and all of their other classes at the same time," says 9th grade biology teacher Debra Franek. Franek, who teaches at West Orange High School in New Jersey, is featured in an online course (cosponsored by the New Jersey Department of Education and Rutgers Continuous Education) titled English

Language Learners in the Mainstream (www.state.nj.us/education/njpep/pd/ell_mainstream).

Franek advises teachers to be flexible when teaching ELLs. She herself adapts the text of her science lessons to help students focus on the essential information for understanding a concept and tells students to stop her if they don't understand a word so that she or a student can illustrate it on the board. Using simple terms can make key science concepts and processes accessible to all students. For example, instead of saying "increase" or "decrease" to signal change, teachers might say "go up" or "go down," and instead of saying "expand" and "contract," they could say "get bigger" or "get smaller."

Franek also presents information visually, through graphs or images on an overhead projector, and even kinesthetically—for example, pointing out different parts of the body. Since becoming aware of visual instructional methods, she has become more animated, drawing and "acting out" more in all her classes. In general, graphics, charts, dictionaries, and just plain old-fashioned body language—hand gestures, facial expressions, and body movements—can help put students at ease and keep communication lines open.

Other strategies to promote science literacy and understanding include using prompts that provide starting points for wording hypotheses (I hypothesize that . . .; When _____ happens, then I predict _____ will occur) and focusing on one or two specific writing objectives for any given assignment (e.g., comparing and contrasting, writing sequential procedures, clear labeling, and so on). During postinvestigation reflections, teachers can foster language generation skills in small-group settings by using timers that allow one minute of talk time per student (Maatta et al., 2006). More than half of Franek's lessons with ELLs involve cooperative learning so that students may readily help one another fill in gaps of understanding.

Studies about teaching science to English language learners consistently focus on hands-on, inquiry-based instruction because it reduces "the language load," points out Okhee Lee. Small-group work during investigations encourages collaboration, modeling of language usage, and conversation. Ideally, during collaboration, Lee says, teachers should permit students to use their home languages so that bilingual students stronger in English can help those with weaker English skills. Although more and more U.S. states seem to be pushing an English-only policy, "teachers ought to allow and encourage the use of home languages," even if only informally, Lee avows. "Otherwise, students just sit there, not knowing what's happening in class."

## The SIOP Model

Professor of special education Jana Echevarria and science education professor Alan Colburn, both from California State University, Long Beach, affirm that "high-quality, hands-on" experiences are the best means of introducing new science concepts and terms to English language learners (Echevarria & Colburn, 2006, p. 95). They show science educators how to carry out inquiry-based science using learning cycle theory combined with the research-based Sheltered Instruction Observation Protocol (SIOP) Model.

The SIOP Model provides teachers with a practical way of conveying content to English language learners by embedding features of high-quality, research-proven ELL instruction. Echevarria, Mary Ellen Vogt, and Deborah Short devised the following eight components of the model as the result of seven years of research:

**1. Preparation:** Clearly state what students ought to know, understand, and be able to do, whether the focus is on science content or English language. Use relevant objects, pictures, and supplementary texts during lessons and pitch the content at an appropriate level for students' grade level and English proficiency. Echevarria recommends using the acronym SWBAT (Students Will Be Able To . . .) to help both teachers and students home in on a lesson's content and language objectives.

**2. Building background:** Link new content with students' prior knowledge.

**3. Comprehensible input:** To aid student understanding, tailor speech, including vocabulary, articulation, and speed of delivery; use multimodal techniques (e.g., drawing, speaking, gesturing, role playing, and so on); and model academic tasks.

**4. Strategies:** Teach, model, and provide scaffolding for academic strategies used by successful learners (e.g., prediction and memory aids).

**5. Interaction:** Encourage both peer-to-peer and student-teacher interaction to give ELLs a chance to use academic language. Sufficient wait time for questions and appropriate student grouping help maximize opportunities for students to convey their knowledge orally.

**6. Practice/Application:** Have students extend their language skills and content knowledge through reading, writing, listening, and speaking.

**7. Lesson delivery:** Carry out a lesson that meets learning objectives and keeps students engaged. Echevarria and Colburn point out that hands-on, inquiry-based lessons provide a vehicle for student engagement and opportunities for talking about their learning.

**8. Review/Assessment:** Determine how well science content goals and language objectives have been met, and give students feedback on their learning. (Echevarria & Colburn, 2006, pp. 99–101)

Echevarria and Colburn point out that the major elements of Robert Karplus's learning cycle, which can be boiled down to *exploration*, *concept introduction*, and *concept application*, easily mesh with the SIOP Model:

• **Exploration** involves hands-on or other stimulating experiences that engage students' senses directly.

• **Concept introduction** may include student discussion of the exploration, while the teacher provides terms to explain the concepts.

• **Concept application** gives opportunities for students to use the new content in other contexts. (DeBoer, 1991, pp. 205–206)

Although science teachers may believe they have little time or expertise to address language objectives for students who are less than proficient in English, ELL experts suggest otherwise—that precisely because students must acquire so much new academic language, science teachers are in a prime position to help students grapple with language to better understand science concepts.

For example, for a middle school science lesson exploring the properties of *ooblek* (a cornstarch mixture that has the properties of both

*continued on page 97*

# Promoting ELLs' Academic Literacy

*Deborah Short and Jana Echevarria*

Our research found that ELLs whose teachers were trained in implementing the SIOP Model performed significantly better on an academic writing assessment than did a comparison group of ELLs whose teachers had had no exposure to the model (Echevarria, Short, & Powers, 2003). Experience with the SIOP Model suggests that the following strategies can help teachers promote academic literacy among English language learners in all subject areas.

Academic literacy refers to the need for students to understand the often dense, expository texts, with their content-specific vocabulary, that are used in math, science, and the social sciences in later elementary school and in secondary school.

**Identify the language demands of the content course.** Content-area teachers should examine their curricula from a language perspective. What aspects of English do students need to know and apply to succeed in the class? For example, does the course require students to write comparison/contrast or problem/solution essays? Read a textbook and take notes? Give oral presentations using technical vocabulary? All these common classroom tasks require facility with academic language. By reflecting on the language demands of their courses, teachers can begin to support students in learning the features of academic English.

**Plan language objectives for all lessons and make them explicit to students.** Although most teachers address content objectives in their lessons, they rarely discuss language objectives—a crucial area for English language learners. Building from an understanding of the language demands of the curriculum, teachers can develop language objectives related to key vocabulary, reading or writing skills, listening or speaking tasks, or language structures. For example, teachers can help students learn to read and write in a specific content area by conducting prereading activities (such as previewing the text chapter by examining the section headings and illustrations) and prewriting activities (such as using sentence starters and graphic organizers to record ideas on a topic).

**Emphasize academic vocabulary development.** Expanding ELLs' academic vocabulary knowledge requires moving beyond the highlighted words in a textbook to include words crucial to conceptual understanding of a topic—not only technical terms but also expressions like *in comparison* and *as a result*, which act like connective tissue in text. Students need multiple opportunities to practice using these words orally and in print. Reading glossary definitions is not sufficient. Strategies such as word walls, semantic webs, and structural analysis can help students organize the new words in meaningful ways. Other vocabulary techniques include demonstrations, illustrations, art projects, and letting students select specific vocabulary words to study.

**Activate and strengthen background knowledge.** Many English language learners struggle with curriculum content because they lack background knowledge of the topic or have gaps in the information they have learned. Teachers must either activate what prior knowledge exists and apply it to lessons or explicitly build background knowledge for these students. When ELLs struggle with schoolwork, teachers should be aware that the problem may be related to background knowledge rather than to intellectual ability. Ask a student from rural Vietnam to write a paragraph about growing rice, and she might have a great deal of information to share from her personal experience; ask her to write about space exploration, and she may have no background knowledge to draw on.

**Promote oral interaction and extended academic talk.** Oral language development can help English language learners acquire literacy skills and access new information. Because much classroom instruction involves discussion, teachers need to encourage ELLs to join in academic talk during class. Teachers should talk less and engage students in extended discussions so that ELLs give more than one-word responses. After a student response, teachers might say, "Tell me more about that" or "Why do you think so?" rather than, "Good. The next question is . . ."

By establishing discussion routines (e.g., asking students to paraphrase one another), teachers provide structures for discussions and teach students to be active listeners. By writing key terms or phrases on the board, teachers give students a resource to use in their own speech. By encouraging ELLs to share their thoughts with a partner before reporting to the whole class, teachers promote both the students' language learning and their confidence in speaking out.

**Review vocabulary and content concepts.** English language learners regularly sit through a 45-minute class period with most of the content provided through a new language. Focusing on instruction delivered through an unfamiliar language all day long is mentally exhausting, and students may find it difficult to identify the most important information among all the ideas conveyed. Teachers should therefore schedule time for review at the end of each lesson, pointing out the key concepts and associated academic vocabulary and making connections to the lesson objectives and state standards. These strategies will help ELLs know what they should study.

**Give students feedback on language use in class.** Content-area teachers are usually skillful in giving feedback to students on their content comprehension but less experienced in giving feedback on the students' language abilities. However, these teachers are in an excellent position to tell students how scientists talk about experimental findings or how historians report on past events. We do not expect content teachers to become linguistic experts, but they can talk explicitly with students about word choice, ways to compare information, and techniques for explaining solutions. Calling attention to language use in content lessons will be valuable to ELLs as they work to develop academic language proficiency.

*Source:* Adapted from "Teacher Skills to Support English Language Learners," by D. Short and J. Echevarria, 2004/2005, *Educational Leadership, 62*(4), pp. 8–13. Copyright © 2004/2005 by Association for Supervision and Curriculum Development.

liquids and solids), content objectives could be that "students will be able to tell how to report the results of scientific research" and draw one or more conclusions, while a language objective could be that "students will report their findings using complete sentences and correct punctuation" (Echevarria & Colburn, 2006, p. 104). Other scaffolding strategies that can help English language learners include prompts in the form of a report outline or graphic organizers.

Jana Echevarria and Deborah Short, who directs the Language Education and Academic Development Division at the Center for Applied Linguistics in Washington, D.C., offer strategies that science and other content-area teachers can use to address students' linguistic needs and to make learning more meaningful (see "Promoting ELLs' Academic Literacy," pp. 94–97).

## Reflections ◆ ◆ ◆

The long-standing problem of getting minority inner-city students to achieve in science needs a new perspective. Science teachers must move away from the traditional approaches of lecture and rote memorization, typical in many urban schools that are under fire for poor academic performance. Some science education researchers are calling for reforms in science teaching that take into consideration the individual circumstances of diverse students. Rather than seeing minority students as having cultural deficits that need "filling up" with lectures and memory drills, educators may find it more effective to first find out what their students know and how they think. When students (and their teachers) realize that they have something to offer and to build on, the possibilities for building bridges to the "culture of science" will be boundless.

# Assessment for Learning 5

*I can't teach them anything—I can only teach them to think.*

—*Socrates*

If education pundits wanted to coin another phrase for a growing problem in education, "assessment wars" might be a good one to bring into currency. In today's climate of accountability, everyone seems to have a different idea of which kinds of assessments will best help students learn. There is, however, one drawback to the term: it's not so clear where the battle lines are drawn, and who's fighting for what. At first glance, on the one side, there are traditional end-of-unit classroom tests and, looming large, institutionalized large-scale normative assessments that have gained the upper hand in an era of accountability. On the other side, there are the formative diagnostic assessments that provide insights into student learning and enable teachers to give students a deeper understanding of classroom knowledge. The two sides seem to be trying to conquer different lands. Or are they? Departments of education, school administrators, teachers, parents, and students themselves need to know that students are in fact learning what they are supposed to be learning and that schools are doing what they are supposed to be doing. But what are the best ways to find out these things?

This chapter takes a look at innovative ways to assess students in science and to address the challenges that districts face in devising good tests to meet the science mandates of No Child Left Behind. After an overview of recent research on formative assessment techniques, the chapter examines how science teachers in one district are moving away from assessments that pressure students into short-term memorization and competition, and toward tests that help students to better understand not only *what* they are learning but also *that* they are learning.

## Better Formative Assessments

In 1998, education researchers Paul Black and Dylan Wiliam published an extensive review of international research literature on formative assessment concluding that using such assessments to tailor instruction can raise student achievement (1998a). Yet they also found that most teachers carry out such assessments poorly, often defaulting to practices that encourage rote learning and competition rather than thoughtful understanding. In a later paper, the researchers identified three main problems: "The first was that the assessment methods that teachers use are not effective in promoting good learning. The second was that marking and grading practices tend to emphasise competition rather than personal improvement. The third problem was that assessment feedback often has a negative impact, particularly on pupils with low attainments who are led to believe that they lack 'ability' and are not able to learn" (Black, Harrison, Lee, Marshall, & Wiliam, 2003).

Black and Wiliam (1998b) criticized the high-stakes standardized tests that dominate teaching and assessment in many nations as "poor models for formative assessment" because of their limited function as mere summaries of achievement rather than helpful diagnoses. But they also believed that changing teaching practices would be difficult because of public policy beliefs and ingrained habits among educators.

Despite such challenges, in a follow-up project carried out by the King's College London Assessment for Learning Group in England, these researchers recruited 36 teachers—24 of whom taught math or science—to integrate certain formative assessment practices in their classrooms. The results led to a new report (Black, Harrison, Lee, Marshall, & Wiliam, 2004) recommending the following in-class assessment practices as powerful ways to improve classroom standards and student performance.

**Questioning.** Increase wait time after questions to at least several seconds to give students room to think. Then use students' answers—whether right or wrong—to develop student understanding. This strategy can also help shift the questioning from fact-finding competitions to exchanges that help students explore deeper content issues.

**Feedback.** Give written feedback that both points out what students have done well and offers guidance on making improvements. Follow up by giving students a chance to respond, and then provide them with time to revise their work based on the feedback. Research shows that when teachers give both written comments and a grade or numerical score, students will focus on the grade and ignore the comments. When teachers in the study decided to use comments alone to assess student work, they found students more enthusiastic about improving their work.

**Self-assessment and peer assessment.** Let students know the criteria for evaluating their learning, then give them opportunities to grade their own and their peers' work. Peer judging, the study found, encourages students to reevaluate their own work more objectively. Teachers taught students to use the effective technique of "traffic light" icons (green for good understanding, yellow for partial understanding, and red for little understanding) to ease them into self-assessment.

**Formative use of summative assessments.** To help students prepare effectively for a test, have them reflect on what they know about key concepts and terms, using such methods as the traffic light technique. Or have students devise possible test questions and grade them so that they better understand the assessment process and where they can improve. Consider letting students apply criteria (even creating a test's scoring rubric) through peer assessment and self-assessment opportunities.

This work could be considered the cutting edge of assessment practice and reform. The preference of formative assessments over high-stakes tests is rare throughout the world. Only the state of Queensland, Australia, has abandoned high-stakes testing requirements for high school graduation and university entry in favor of teacher assessment of student portfolios (Black et al., 2003), and it took several years of professional development to alter that state's assessment practices. Black and Wiliam (2004) describe the multistep process involved: "First, they needed help to break their initial reliance on the types of test that the earlier external test system used. Second, they needed to develop formative skills, in part so that they were better able to guide and judge students' use of portfolios. Third, they needed to develop the procedures and skills for the conduct of moderation meetings at which samples of student portfolios have to be exchanged between teachers to help arrive at agreement on common standards" (p. 29).

The authors' suggestions are doable, but they require both teachers and students to learn new skills that involve better monitoring of progress through a variety of formal and informal ongoing assessments that reveal student understanding over time. When teachers (and even trained peers) provide students with specific feedback and guidance on how to improve their work and reach their goals for a particular assignment, student engagement and understanding increase.

## Science Notebooks in the Lab and in the Classroom

One way for teachers to conduct ongoing assessments while helping students to make connections between science and literacy is to have students keep science notebooks, similar to those used by professional scientists. With appropriate adaptations for different grade levels, the science notebook becomes a reflective tool that makes use of the learning principles outlined in cognitive science research. Oklahoma-based science reform consultant Sande Sparkman finds that distributing copies of a working scientist's laboratory notebook drives home to teachers the value that science professionals place in putting their thinking on paper. Student science notebooks are open-ended and the antithesis of worksheets, which typically call for low levels of knowledge, Sparkman tells teachers: "Responses in a notebook or journal, when an appropriate prompt is given, require students to think, analyze, and respond to information. This requires students' deeper understanding of concepts and analysis of thoughts about those concepts." Students learn not only to collect evidence for an investigation but also to defend their own results, as opposed to merely verifying someone else's learning via a cookbook lab.

By thinking on paper, Sparkman adds, students also draw connections to larger scientific ideas beyond the specific concept being addressed in the lesson. Students, like scientists, can use notebooks to raise questions, document procedures, collect data, and write conclusions. These activities directly engage students in understanding the nature of science. Perusing the professional scientist's notebook conveys an especially important fact to teachers: science is a human activity done by real people, not fill-in-the-blank exercises that demand one right answer. "The students should learn to use these notebooks the way a scientist does: to clarify thinking, to ask questions, to share with others, to find holes in their thinking, and to justify their thought processes," says Sparkman.

In her professional development sessions, Sparkman asks teachers to document the kinds of information they find in a sample research scientist's notebooks. Along with the elements of experimental design, teachers find drawings, notes on procedural mistakes (and the reasons for them), crossed-out sentences, cross-references, and reflections on prior work of other scientists. When teachers remark on the legibility of some notebooks, Sparkman informs them that professional scientists must keep handwritten notes for patent purposes and record times of discoveries to solidify their claims on knowledge: "In business and industry, the pursuit is dollars. Dollars come from patents," says Sparkman, who has worked as a chemist. While the goal of science notebooks is not to create patents, they do allow science students to generate "a similar atmosphere of questioning, data collection, data analysis, and defense of the analysis."

## Tips on Using Science Notebooks

Notebooks also provide science teachers with a ready gauge of learning in the classroom. If teachers check students' notebooks on a regular basis—say, collecting the notebooks of five students each week—they can find out what students know and what they still need to learn. Sparkman also advises teachers to

• Grade notebooks only for participation so that students' sense of ownership is not compromised.

• Check notebooks as students are on the way out the door so that they can adjust their instruction for the next day.

• Allow students to use their notebooks during test reviews and tests and to consult the notebooks when completing homework or responding to questions and prompts during class.

• Encourage self-evaluation. For example, teachers may ask students to pick their "best" work, whether it's data collection, a written assignment, or a graphical representation of data. Then they can have students self-assess what the "best" means in the case of each choice.

Sparkman emphasizes that "self-reflection is the key to learning. From novice to expert, the key factor is that the expert sees, feels, and knows the patterns." Teachers can provide prompts about such patterns (e.g., the differences in life cycles among plants, invertebrates, and mammals) to help students aspire to the expert's deeper understanding.

Peer assessments of notebooks also have great value, Sparkman notes. While passing notebooks during a round-robin session, for example, students can look for the best aspects of another student's notebook and explain why. This process helps students better discern what needs improving in their own notebooks and get ideas for improvement. When students see areas they can improve, or find out how others looked at an investigation in a different way, they become more objective about their own work.

Notebook assignments can be assessed formatively, and it's the teacher's responsibility to create appropriate measures for them, says Sparkman. A rubric should address the concept development of a lesson and allow students to assess their own learning. Taking the time to appraise their learning lets students "own the information" and enables them to draw connections to the larger ideas in science, Sparkman says. She advises teachers to let students help craft the rubric. When the class goes through the process of creating a rubric, students who are unsure of what is required can listen to other students who do understand: "My experience was that the conversation allowed a window for those lower-level students to understand expectations through the eyes of their peers," notes Sparkman.

Sparkman finds that the process of developing the rubric works best when teachers reserve the right to decide "at least 50 percent" of the rubric so that they can tailor challenges for a range of students, especially those with the greatest learning needs. She observes, "It's not a challenge to take good students and keep them good! Truly great teachers take those who are not doing so well and give them the skills, knowledge, and confidence to come up to the level of the good students."

## Widening the Scope of Formative Assessment

Teachers of Westside High School's Natural Science course, open to 9th and 10th graders, want to be certain that they are helping their students succeed in learning science concepts. A variety of formative assessments helps these teachers keep a daily pulse on students' learning.

Borrowing from assessment guru Rick Stiggins the idea that students can hit any target they see as long as it stays constant, Westside's Michael Fryda ensures that his course sets out (1) clear knowledge standards and (2) expectations for using the standards of critical thought (see p. 56) to communicate in the spoken and the written word. "All of our written and oral feedback about student work stems from these two sources. Students know from day one what we expect of them," Fryda says.

Creating and using a variety of assessments for learning is another of Stiggins's ideas used in Westside's science classrooms. Teams of teachers have created teacher's guides to be used with open-ended oral and written questions that assess students' daily learning. The guide reminds teachers to give students "some tough love" by not accepting low-quality work. Low quality, the guide explains, manifests itself as incomplete assignments, incomplete sentences, or "no thought about the question reflected by nonsensical responses." In addition, the Natural Science course includes lab exercises, performance-based projects, and exams that give students multiple opportunities to demonstrate their understanding in ways that suit the content as well as their learning styles, Fryda points out.

Fryda and other Natural Science teachers have also adopted the assessment and grading practices of Canadian educator Ken O'Connor, an expert on assessment for learning. One of these practices involves selecting only a few assignments for grading, although all student work is evaluated. To spell out the difference between formative and summative assessments to students, "we explain that some assignments are practice for learning while others are demonstrations of learning and count toward their grade," Fryda says. Another important grading practice appeals to teenagers' sense of justice while keeping their focus on learning: "We don't mix behaviors like tardiness, absenteeism, work completion, or effort with measures of academic achievement. Instead, we evaluate behavior and academic achievement separately because we want to know what students really do know and understand about science," Fryda stresses. Three key factors guide formative assessments at Westside:

**1. The assessments use an equal-interval grading scale—1, 2, 3, 4, 5—instead of traditional percentages.** This scale accurately averages the trend of student work, says Fryda, while avoiding the traditional grade scale that overpunishes students for missed assignments even when the rest of the evidence (for example, work completion or class participation) shows that they have mastered the content.

**2. Teachers don't give zeros for work not completed.** Avoiding the use of zeros keeps students focused on their work rather than on potential punishments. "Our change in focus has for the most part eliminated the learned helplessness that commonly challenges low-performing students who, under traditional grading systems, simply give up when they realize that several zeros doom their chances of getting anything but a *D* or an *F*," Fryda asserts.

Careful use of encouraging language in the classroom helps students quickly learn that although the formative assessments "don't count," they can help teachers diagnose what students know and understand,

Fryda says. Teachers liberally record "incompletes" to send the message that they care deeply about students always having another chance to demonstrate their learning, he adds.

**3. Teachers don't accept student work until it meets the "high-quality work" standard.** "We want students to realize that formative assessments are valuable learning tools that help them do better on summative assessments. Because of our changes in grading and assessment, we are confident that our student grades tell us whether or not students met the standards being taught," Fryda affirms.

## Technology for Testing

Students in science classes at Westside High School call it "that clicker game." What they're referring to is the Classroom Performance System (CPS), a remote control system that teachers use for formative assessments.

CPS allows students to "click in" answers to multiple-choice questions presented on a projection system and receive immediate feedback on how accurately they and their classmates responded. Students are not individually identified to their classmates; instead, answers are linked to the numbering system on their clickers, which only the teacher knows. "Anonymity removes much of the fear of volunteering during a class for students, and they love this method of receiving feedback," says Fryda. "For students to provide accurate feedback on what they know and understand, they have to feel that they can do so without fear of ridicule or embarrassment."

In addition to encouraging "shy or fearful students" to break out of their shells and get engaged with questions that shape their learning, Fryda adds, teachers benefit because they get a true snapshot of what students know. On the basis of that picture, made in what Fryda calls "academic safety," teachers can then make decisions about tailoring teaching both to the whole class and to individual students. "It's been an invaluable tool for formative assessment," Fryda attests.

## NCLB Science Testing: Its Promise and Peril

NCLB-mandated science testing is the latest piece of the science education reform puzzle. As state education officials assess their design approaches to newly minted or revised annual assessments, the big question on education reformers' minds is, Can such state science testing be approached as business as usual?

Most educators agree that standardized tests have a limited capacity to convey what students know. The shortcomings of a 60-minute paper-and-pencil exam become even more apparent when it comes to science, researchers say.

"Critical aspects of science—inquiry, for example—cannot be well measured or well assessed on a single, time-limited test," says Meryl Bertenthal, coeditor of *Systems for State Science Assessment*. That report, the culmination of a two-year $1.8 million National Research Council study, offers state education departments suggestions to help them reassess K–12 science testing under NCLB.

Science education researchers, like Bertenthal, have high hopes that upcoming tests will at least mark the beginning of change in how schools assess science—and ultimately influence curriculum and instruction. Whittling down and streamlining the science standards could only help the cause of learning science, the report concludes: "A potentially positive outcome of a reorganization in state standards from discrete topics to big ideas is a shift from breadth of coverage to depth of coverage around a relatively small set of foundational principles" (Wilson & Bertenthal, 2005, p. 3).

### Classroom-Level Assessments

To test inquiry—that central component of good science teaching—*Systems for State Science Assessment* encourages states to consider creating a system of multiple tests that assess students' abilities to frame appropriate questions for investigation, make predictions, and evaluate claims on the basis of evidence. One such test might be a classroom assessment that teachers could conduct over a longer stretch of time than one class period.

"Teachers could observe students doing an inquiry and evaluate their work as they continue it," Meryl Bertenthal says. "So much science requires revision and rethinking. You're gathering evidence to see what that tells you, then trying to synthesize and pull things together. That's really hard to capture on a multiple-choice test." She notes that "right now there's no ready mechanism for recording these kinds of assessments into the scores reported as part of NCLB." Nonetheless, Bertenthal says, although standardized classroom-level assessments may be hard to implement in the short term, states should eventually make them part of a system of multiple science assessments.

## Aligning Tests with Standards

According to NCLB, state assessments must be aligned with learning standards. This requirement compels states to take a hard look at how they select and organize those standards.

Typically, state science standards overwhelm educators with a welter of topic-based information to teach—mostly disconnected facts, formulas, and procedures. The study committee behind *Systems for State Science Assessment* wants this to change, suggesting that standards—and therefore instruction and testing—should help students focus on big ideas in science (Wilson & Bertenthal, 2005).

Although *Benchmarks for Science Literacy* has mapped out learning progressions for major science concepts, further research is necessary to determine the age-appropriate introduction of material recommended by standards documents (Smith, Wiser, Anderson, Krajcik, & Coppola, 2004). States also need to solve the potential problem of the disconnect between the "cognitive demands" of the standards and the reality of the actual test, says Bertenthal. "In science, a lot of standards ask that students be able to analyze, understand, conduct, *do* things," she points out, but standardized tests tend to take the low cognitive road of "identifying, defining, and calculating."

It's unlikely that most states will iron out all these issues in the early rounds of state science testing, but as testing continues and "states have time to think about it," the recommendations of *Systems for State Science Assessment* will have more influence and be more useful, says Bertenthal.

Nebraska, for one, has devolved decision making about NCLB-mandated science testing to local school districts—a situation viewed as a boon by many science teachers in the state. Westside Community Schools, a small district of just over 6,000 students, has chosen to create its own science assessment for its high school rather than opt for a commercially produced test. See "Rolling with the NCLB Assessment: Keeping Responsibility at the Local Level" for Michael Fryda's take on this decision.

## Rolling with the NCLB Assessment: Keeping Responsibility at the Local Level

*Michael Fryda*

No matter how you feel about No Child Left Behind (NCLB) and its implementation, I think all educators can agree that we need to hold ourselves accountable for doing the best we can to help students learn. Nebraska has treated NCLB as an opportunity to critically assess our abilities and practices in education. We are convinced that if we strive to improve student learning, we will end up meeting NCLB requirements without forcing the practice of "teaching to the test" into our pedagogy.

Looking for better ways to organize curriculum and to teach and assess students are things all teachers should be doing, regardless of whether the government mandates it. I believe that. I also believe that any individual teacher, school, district, or state can meet the high-stakes expectations of NCLB by following the research-based suggestions of education scholars. The work will be challenging, but if we go about it in a stressed and reactionary manner, we certainly will be neither productive nor successful.

My advice to colleagues in the field is to think past your original training. We all learn "efficient" ways to do things in our teacher training programs. Many time-tested traditions of education are still worthwhile. Some are outdated. Yet we cannot afford to assume that just because we have been doing something a certain way for 40 years, we are doing it the best way or the only way. Teachers need to ask themselves if the way they are assessing students makes sense. What are you assessing? Is what you are assessing really what students must know to be successful in the future? What message are you sending to your students when you assess in a certain way?

Like many teachers, I struggle with the idea that different can be better. Change is hard, and the struggle of taking the first step to change is the hardest one. But as professionals, we can't be afraid to make decisions when they are based on strong research.

Fortunately, even in the accountability era, Nebraska trusts its teachers. Nebraska acknowledges that we are highly gifted professionals and experts in our content areas and puts the power to create accurate NCLB assessments into the hands of teachers in individual districts. This, more than anything, shows that the state recognizes that we are in the best position to make decisions for our schools and students.

In practice, this delegation of responsibility means that each district can either choose to write its own highly accurate criterion-referenced assessments or adopt one or more outside tests. Many districts, including mine, have chosen the former. I sat on the committee that wrote our district assessments for the biology and the Science, Society, and Technology standards and cochaired the committees that wrote our district assessments for earth and space science. In all cases, we worked closely with our district assessment director to make sure that our tests are written at the appropriate reading level and that they are reliable, valid, and free of bias. We are still beta-testing and refining these assessments, but we will be reporting results to the state for the first time in 2008.

Writing these assessments has encouraged our own science department to take a hard look at our overall course structure. As a result of this self-evaluation, we decided to add an additional earth and space science course to be absolutely certain that students learn all our standards, regardless of which curriculum pathway they

> choose to follow. NCLB testing indirectly led to that decision. Yet we are doing it not because we are required to, but because we think it's in the best interest of student learning.

One advantage of a district-created test is that district science educators know their students and the particular groups of students that will find certain test questions difficult or easy, says Fryda. Test-writing teams rank-order questions for each test into four categories: "beginning," "progressing," "proficient," and "advanced."

"From an assessment perspective, you would want each category to get about equal weight in terms of number of questions," Fryda points out. During the test-writing process, a few challenges cropped up: teachers "agonized" over the division of questions between the "progressing" and "proficient" categories, and they discovered that they had more questions on the "proficient" and "advanced" end of the scale than on the lower end. "We were concerned that for students who were in the 'beginning' category, there would not be enough questions for them to answer, so we would be misidentifying them," he says.

While Westside teachers want to make sure that they don't create too difficult a test that would result in an inaccurate picture of students' learning, they also want to balance the questions' challenge levels without removing rigor. "That's a really difficult thing to do sometimes. We don't want to soften the test, but we just want to change the focus of the test to make sure we have more of a representation from 'beginning' all the way to 'advanced.' It's a continual process [of revision]. Sometimes it's not until students take the test that you can really know what they find difficult," Fryda explains.

The modes of assessment reflect what teachers want to know about student learning. For example, the biology assessment and the Science, Society, and Technology assessment both ask for short-answer or written responses. "In order for students to really show what they know and understand, they have to be able to write a narrative about it," Fryda explains. On the other hand, the earth and space science assessment is multiple-choice because it is "a straight-up" content assessment. "We're really just interested in whether or not [students] can show us their knowledge and understanding based upon selecting from a variety of choices," he says.

The inquiry assessment is "heavily written," says Fryda, because it's testing students' ability to design and execute an experiment and to collect and present data. For this test, students are given the real-world problem of designing a new carnival attraction—taking into consideration such factors as motion, velocity, gravity, and acceleration—for which they must first design experiments that inform their recommendations.

This test has all the elements of an inquiry experience: stating the purpose, writing a series of hypotheses and questions to investigate, writing the procedures to demonstrate understanding of the processes of science, and writing out data tables or creating graphs to present and interpret the data. There's a "tremendous amount of writing," Fryda says. The 9th graders who take Natural Science have a week to take the inquiry assessment. "We can fit it into a time frame that we deem appropriate, so they can show us what they really understand," Fryda asserts.

All students at Westside are required to take all four components of the science assessment—biology; Science, Society, and Technology; earth and space science; and inquiry—before they graduate from high school, but certain tests are tied to certain required classes in the science curriculum. So the earth and space science assessment and the inquiry assessment, which has a physics content base, can be given during Natural Science or physics. The biology assessment and the Science, Society, and Technology assessment are given during biology. The distribution of the testing among different courses spreads the burden over time so that teachers don't feel they have to teach to the test, Fryda explains.

## Trying to Make Ends Meet

Veteran science teacher and science department chair Robert Martin worries that the seriousness of the Maryland High School Assessment (HSA), slated for algebra, biology, and English, has not quite dawned on students at Fairmont Heights High School in Prince George's County, Maryland. The school, whose student body is mostly African American, is located in the inner suburbs of Washington, D.C.

The state evaluations and the public perception of the school are pretty much based on the school's performance on these tests, Martin says. "We're still having trouble with students not grasping that this is a graduation requirement. There's still this attitude that this is just another class and that this test isn't going to matter, so why work hard?"

It's a cause for concern. Although 78 percent of students in Fairmont's biotechnology magnet program passed an earlier pilot assessment in biology, only about 20 percent of the rest of the students—two-thirds of the student population—got passing marks. "The biotech kids are different. A lot of them are interested in medicine and forensics," Martin adds. But among most students at Fairmont, science does not register a strong following. "We're still struggling to get them to pass," he says.

The contrast between the mainstream students and those in the biotech program is only too obvious to Martin. "A lot of students have been turned off to science before they get here, so it's hard to get them back. They're just waiting to get their three science credits and do something else," says Martin. "There is a problem getting students to realize that there are a lot of jobs they can go into with science. A lot of students don't see themselves going into that field or being qualified to go into that field."

Fairmont is thus charged with the difficult task of raising science achievement among low achievers while simultaneously engaging and stimulating higher achievers. The school tackles this challenge both by providing a highly structured science curriculum and by opening its rigorous biotechnology magnet program to any interested students.

Fairmont's general science program uses curriculum frameworks tied to each science subject. These highly detailed documents give practically minute-by-minute breakdowns of what teachers and students should be doing to cover content and carry out labs and other exercises in a 90-minute period. Researchers and teachers themselves admit that such plans put instructors in a bind because they tend to be viewed as scripted lessons that can't be modified. In addition, "because teachers don't have to grapple with their own understanding of the content as they plan a lesson, they tend to not see the connections between the content and the unifying themes of science," suggests science education professor Gale Seiler, who has seen this happen with new teachers in Baltimore's schools.

Fairmont teachers regularly conduct formative assessments to gauge students' understanding. For example, the Classroom Performance System enables teachers to conduct real-time assessments during lessons, gaining feedback on objective questions instantaneously through handheld wireless "clickers" in which students log their answers. These instantly tabulated responses tell teachers where student understanding is strong and where it is weak and enable them to tailor their instruction accordingly. In addition to these high-tech formative assessments, "we have chapter tests for each chapter in biology. These are all graded and categorized by topic, and analyzed so we know which topics the students got and which ones they didn't. There's a lot of data analysis going on," Martin states.

Prince George's County Public Schools has also trained teachers to instruct students in test-taking techniques. For example, practicing brief constructed responses teaches students to include salient information in their short-paragraph answers, a format used in the state examination. Teachers require students to use this format in their daily routines, and further practice takes place during quarterly benchmark assessments that prepare students for the state exam.

On the flip side of this highly structured curriculum is Fairmont's open-enrollment biotech program. One of two such magnet programs in the county, it serves about 300 highly motivated 9th–12th graders. Students in this college prep program undergo a rigorous science and math program and take advantage of the school's science labs, which Martin calls the "best in the county." Fairmont's equipment even includes an electron microscope, which students learn to use starting in 9th grade.

Students also discuss controversial topics in biotechnology—such as genetic engineering, cloning, and stem cell research—and how laws are being written to address them. Martin emphasizes to students that they will be the ones making decisions about these issues in the near future. These discussions give students a broader understanding of science's effect on society; some students even become interested in pursuing law, Martin notes.

## Working with What You've Got

The Missouri Assessment Program (MAP) was one of the first state assessments approved for use under the No Child Left Behind science testing mandate. The MAP's inquiry-based component—about 30 percent of the test—has been around for at least 15 years, says high school science teacher Paula Young. Any inquiry-based activities in class can only benefit students in such an assessment, she says.

Although Missouri had piloted hands-on performance assessments for science, these proved too costly for large-scale tests. Instead, the science assessment uses *performance events*, which give students written scenarios that may require them to analyze events, work with data, interpret graphs, and draw conclusions to show their understanding of some of the process skills of inquiry. For example, "students might be asked to determine a problem, write a testable question, and then design the procedures for an investigation," Young says.

Mapping curriculum so tightly that a teacher's individuality or special talent is neutralized is "a crime," asserts Young. Although she concedes that some test preparation is unavoidable, and can even help to raise scores, Young insists that an effective teacher can develop inquiry-based activities that meet state objectives while engaging students. Missouri hosts the Web-based SuccessLink (www.successlink.org) as a resource for its time-strapped teachers to find or submit such model lessons. In addition, groups of teachers have been working as professional learning communities to develop model formative and summative assessments for different science classes.

"The test formats have, unfortunately, taken the form of multiple-choice questions and state assessment–type questions," Young says, because that's what students will be dealing with. "Such ongoing assessments at least give the teacher the opportunity to know what we need to improve in teaching prior to students taking the state assessments," she notes. In an ideal world, formative assessments would have a hands-on component, "but if our goal is to prepare them for the state assessment, which doesn't have a hands-on component, I guess we're doing the best we can."

## Reflections ◆ ◆ ◆

The recent ushering of science education into the age of accountability brings pluses and minuses. Making sure that schools give all students a solid understanding of science is a praiseworthy yet difficult goal. Every educator knows that the reductionism of teaching to the test is counterproductive to learning. Nevertheless, large-scale assessments are forcing many schools to look afresh at how they assess students. A positive outcome may be that schools and teachers find better and alternative ways to use formative assessments to improve student learning.

The chapter's opening forecast of impending assessment wars could perhaps be downgraded to a summons for an "assessment struggle" to be played out internally within states, school districts, and schools, as well as within the practice of teachers themselves, as each seeks the best ways to get an honest picture of student understanding.

# 6

# Implications for Professional Development

*We're never going to get anywhere as a nation if professional development is for volunteers.*

—Iris Weiss

Science education researcher and former high school biology teacher Iris Weiss knows a lot about professional development. She and colleagues conducted a study sponsored by the National Science Foundation called *Lessons from a Decade of Mathematics and Science Reform* (Banilower, Boyd, Pasley, & Weiss, 2006). The study synthesizes the evidence of 75,000 math and science teachers who cumulatively took part in 88 professional development programs over a 10-year period. The programs were part of the NSF's Local Systemic Change through Teacher Enhancement initiative.

The study's findings confirm to Weiss that when schools promote "a critical mass of teachers engaging in the same enterprise," discourse about changing science and math does make a difference in teaching and learning in those subjects. "You're not just getting professional development during the formal workshop. You're also getting professional development when teachers talk to each other about their practice—with a focus on learning goals," Weiss observes. "All kids deserve to learn science from well-prepared teachers. Why should it be up to the teacher to decide whether or not to get professional development?"

Limited time and resources seems to be the biggest hurdle for science teachers to overcome in getting the professional development they need to improve their teaching and grow in their careers. Some teachers are able to work together in professional learning communities, attend NSTA and other science education conferences, participate in Web-based seminars, work with professional scientists, and take courses at local colleges and universities. Other teachers make do with routine inservice programs. The needs of struggling science teachers, especially novices, are extensive. In these cases, ongoing mentoring provides a forum for getting sound advice on content and classroom management issues as well as a safe haven for venting typical new-teacher frustrations with the status quo.

In this chapter, science educators offer ideas and strategies to help teachers reexamine their understanding of scientific inquiry and to give them fresh insight into their approach to this central practice of science. The chapter also explores effective types of professional development for teachers at different stages in their science teaching careers.

## How's Your Inquiry These Days?

As we saw in Chapter 1, scientific inquiry seems to take on different shapes depending on whether it's in a classroom or in a real-life science laboratory, partly because the two worlds of school and professional science research only rarely break bread together.

"The majority of science teachers have never actually done scientific work outside of the classroom. This leaves them in a position to imagine much about this work with only minimal experiences to support those imaginations," asserts Stephen Thompson, assistant professor of science education in the Department of Instruction and Teacher Education at the University of South Carolina.

Thompson's inquiry framework, introduced in Chapter 1 (see Figure 1.1, p. 9), can be a means for teachers to see where their beliefs and practices fit on the spectrum of scientific inquiry. Groups of science teachers can use the matrix to discuss how they can help students understand the key ideas and the complexities of inquiry. Professional development workshops may build science teachers' content knowledge or pedagogical practices, but they won't necessarily help teachers understand how scientists work and what factors influence that work, Thompson says.

"Knowing this should change the way that professional development for science teachers is approached," Thompson observes. He suggests that "rather than sending science teachers to workshops that are content-based or focused on instructional techniques, the principal or science chair might focus professional development activities on enhancing understandings related to scientific inquiry and the nature of science."

Thompson himself was a middle school science teacher for six years before realizing that "my ideas about scientific inquiry were naïve," he recalls. After Thompson spent a summer conducting meteorological research with scientists at a local university, he better understood that scientific inquiry went way beyond the confines of the five-step scientific method. He urges schools, as resource strapped as they may be, to find ways to help science teachers collaborate with working scientists for professional development, or to develop a plan to get scientists to take an active role as regular guests in their science classrooms.

In addition to Thompson's inquiry framework, Rebecca Reiff's inquiry wheel, also featured in Chapter 1 (see Figure 1.2, p. 13), is another tool that can convey to science teachers how scientists understand and practice inquiry. Reiff says that teacher educators have found the model helpful for opening up discussions about the nature of science and its processes because of the wheel's depiction of the "evolving process of scientific investigations."

Reiff hopes that this dynamic depiction of inquiry, developed using research scientists' own descriptions of their work, will foster "a different tone" in science classes by keeping questions at the center and encouraging students to "take an active role in participating in science learning" (Reiff, 2005).

## Mentoring Science Teachers

New or struggling science teachers often need to focus on the nuts and bolts of instruction, such as selecting engaging ways to convey content or organizing labs efficiently. As a mentor teacher in science and math for Prince George's County Public Schools in Maryland, Jaimie Foster helps novice and struggling teachers improve their instructional practice and reinforces what she knows herself: that science teaching is a rewarding career. Foster, who taught chemistry and biology for seven years, observes that "to be truly successful, it takes planning, preparation, and a desire to step outside the box."

One of the schools Foster works with is Fairmont Heights High School. Fairmont is an intriguing study in contrasts. Students in the school's biotechnology magnet program, about one-third of the total enrollment, are motivated to do well in science and have career ambitions in science or health-related fields. Yet according to standardized test results in reading and math, Fairmont is among the lowest-performing schools in the county, and most students have failed pilot versions of the state science assessment. That makes science teachers' jobs—and Foster's job—even more difficult.

"A number of the students are below grade level in reading, math, and critical thinking skills—three vital components for all science courses. That alone can be especially challenging for a science educator," Foster attests. In addition, "most science teachers need help with instruction, lab management, and getting enough confidence to try new skills or activities." Yet despite such challenges, Foster maintains that teachers who reflect on their instruction and persevere in the classroom can find ways to engage even the most challenging students.

Foster is especially keen on moving teachers beyond the old-school standbys of lectures and worksheets to inquiry-based teaching that gives students a larger role in their learning. To jump-start inquiry-based practices in the classroom, Foster gives teachers the following important advice: "Do not be afraid to allow students to feel comfortable to make mistakes. There are usually several ways to a right answer—let them figure it out!" She tells teachers that inquiry-based teaching can begin by simply encouraging students to use their senses to identify basic properties of sample elements, such as color, texture, or magnetic ability. She encourages teachers to let go, so that students become the ones asking the questions, posing the problems, and looking for solutions.

Because students are at varying levels of reading comprehension and math skills, Foster advises teachers on different ways to present science concepts. Varying the types of learning activities provides multiple entry points to the topic.

For example, combining computer simulations with lab investigations can help prepare students for hands-on work and make scientific processes seem less abstract. "In learning to balance equations, one group may be completing a microscale lab of mixing reactions and identifying the products based on the physical evidence seen. Another group may be on the computer manipulating a simulation of a fetal pig dissection, while a third is doing pencil-and-paper balancing and identifying of chemical equations," Foster explains.

Foster works with teachers to develop multiple activities to appeal to students' different modes of learning. For example, various hands-on activities can be used to explore mitosis, including drawing pictures of the stages of cell division; constructing models of dividing cells and nuclei with yarn, glue, and construction paper; or playing the "mitosis memory game," which has students match a verbal description of the phase with its scientific name.

## Science Confidential

Jaimie Foster and her fellow mentor Joan Newton, a retired science teacher, are visiting their mentees during a high-pressure week at Fairmont. In 10th grade biology classes, teachers are helping students review for a benchmark test that will address that quarter's content on cellular respiration, photosynthesis, and genetics. The material will also be a part of the upcoming Maryland High School Assessment in biology.

After observing one new teacher's self-contained biology class of about eight male students, Foster arranges to confer with the teacher later that morning. The teacher's instructor-centered approach consists of asking the students questions and filling out their partial responses with her own definitions read from a sheet. The review of cellular respiration and photosynthesis moves at a snail's pace, with some students arriving late and others resting their heads on their desks. When one student suggests that they play a review game, the teacher willingly takes up his idea and writes terms on the chalkboard for students to identify, such as *Krebs cycle, electron transport chain,* and *mitochondrion.* This review fares no better, however, so the teacher distributes the county's review guide and asks students to read over the relevant sections for homework.

Foster uses an observation rubric to mark what was positive and what could use improvement in the teacher's presentation of content. She marks "differentiated instruction" and "use manipulatives" on her chart as practices that the teacher should incorporate and notes that the teacher also needs help with her lesson planning and execution.

During their conference, Foster tells the new teacher that the game "could have been an awesome way to review" and recommends that the teacher prepare better next time by creating the game beforehand. Foster suggests a Monopoly-style game in which students would have the option to buy "properties," such as Mitochondria Place or Chloroplast Avenue, when they correctly answer questions about key science terms. Foster also suggests retrieving the three-dimensional cell model that the teacher has used in previous classes to review key cell parts. The model reinforces understanding by appealing to students' visual and tactile learning modalities.

Foster worries that some county science teachers she works with may see the district's highly detailed curriculum framework progress guide as the formula for scripted lessons. So while pointing out that the district has designated the curriculum framework as the most efficient way to teach the material, Foster suggests that the teacher use the framework more as a guide to develop her own creative lesson plans. "You need to go where your kids are at and at the pace they can maintain," Foster advises her.

For example, to help special-needs students complete the curriculum framework's activity on mitosis and meiosis ("Complete mitosis/meiosis lab in order for students to compare/contrast the stages of each cell division type"), Foster suggests that the teacher allow students to take time to draw the stages of each type of cell division to reinforce the contrasting stages in their minds.

During the observation, the new teacher handled class management issues by sending troublemakers to the principal's office. Foster provides alternatives more in line with the school's obligation and goal to teach every student. "Kids need to understand that teachers want to work with them," she notes, and the teacher can communicate this with an encouraging side comment, a private conference after class, or a discreet signal that can cue the student to redirect his behavior.

Foster tells the teacher that some of the more motivated boys in the class should be recruited to help peer-teach the others. She also suggests that the teacher hold a meeting with a particular student and his father to work together to improve his behavior and performance in class. The teacher will also consider inviting students to negotiate "behavioral contracts," which could stipulate, for example, that to be guaranteed a *C*, the student must agree to arrive on time to class, complete all homework, maintain on-task behavior, and score 70 percent or higher on all quizzes and tests.

The teacher, reinvigorated by Foster's support, appears ready to face the challenges of teaching for the next semester. Foster promises the teacher that she will check in on her class the following month.

## From Manila to Maryland

Fairmont's biology review moves along more smoothly in another class, although the teacher must deal with such off-task behavior as students loudly calling out to one another and jumping out of their seats. Ann Marie De Peralta arrived from the Philippines three months earlier to take over this biology course, whose original teacher abruptly left. Because of the scarcity of math and science teachers willing to teach in low-performing schools, Fairmont Heights High School—like a growing number of inner-city schools throughout the United States—has hired nonnative teachers to teach these key subjects. The combination of urban youth and foreign teachers can prove difficult: standard classroom management issues are exacerbated by cultural differences, unfamiliar accents, and the more traditional teaching styles of the overseas teachers, who tend to be unused to the often chaotic inner-city classrooms.

De Peralta is a "floater." A teacher without a classroom, she must wheel a cart containing a class set of textbooks and her own materials from room to room. Because she has taught biology for five years in her home country, De Peralta's content knowledge and teaching experience help her to keep the attention of the class. It is a struggle at times.

For example, because students constantly chatter, De Peralta ends up straining her voice to be heard over the noise of the class. Yet she keeps students moving through a 20-question multiple-choice review covering material that they will be tested on later in the week.

De Peralta observes that her students are accustomed to written work and prefer worksheets in line with their previous school experiences, so it's hard to get their attention when such routines are changed. To start off class, De Peralta has adopted the use of a daily warm-up paper that students fill in with the main objectives of the day and two vocabulary words related to the Maryland High School Assessment. De Peralta typically uses PowerPoint slides to alert students to that day's warm-up material.

It's a good strategy. "Usually when students come in, they're all hyper. If they know there's a routine, that they have to settle down and write that day's objectives and do the warm-up—that helps," explains Joan Newton, her faculty mentor.

De Peralta also feels free to rewrite the standard science worksheets to make the information hang together more easily. "I want them to remember concepts easily. I try to make everything connected in a worksheet, so I give them concept maps and lots of illustrations because today's generation are visual thinkers," she says.

Sometimes it's a matter of demystifying the heavily Greek- and Latin-based vocabulary of biology. For example, to convey the concept of *phagocytosis*—the cell's process of consuming food particles or foreign bodies—De Peralta just gives students the literal translation from the Greek: "It's the cell eating process." This renaming captures the larger idea and prevents students from getting bogged down with the details of parroting the definition, she says. Before students explore further, De Peralta stimulates their imaginations by asking them to think about what a cell could eat and how it might happen.

She also tries to make the structure and functions of the cell parts a bit more concrete in students' minds, asking them to recall certain features of the cell by drawing an analogy to their own classroom: the classroom walls stand in for the cell membrane, the door is a protein that allows the diffusion of certain substances through the membrane, and the classroom number stands for the carbohydrates that act as markers for the cell type, De Peralta tells the class.

Today, the system of handheld clickers that allows De Peralta to immediately gauge student understanding is not functioning, which is why she is handing out review worksheets instead of using an overhead computer screen. But De Peralta uses technology in other ways, including today's computer simulation of meiosis and mitosis and virtual labs, which are occasionally done because the lab materials and lab space are not always available.

In a conversation with Newton, De Peralta discusses her practice and mentions that she might incorporate pop music as a hook into her teaching and classroom management. The other day, she directed students' attention to some organelles in a diagram of a cell by singing "to the left, to the left"—a refrain from "Irreplaceable," a song by hip-hop diva Beyoncé Knowles. That made students laugh, De Peralta says. Newton agrees that even such small efforts to connect with teenage students' lives are worthwhile.

The modeling that Foster and Newton provide to inexperienced or struggling science teachers can be crucial steps in laying the groundwork for a teaching career or in getting up to speed on new instructional strategies. A way to continue the positive effects of such modeling and support takes the form of the regular exchanges, observations, and critiques offered by professional learning communities.

## Professional Learning Communities

Omaha's Westside High School has retained some aspects of its 1960s modular scheduling, which has proved to be a boon for the development of the science department's professional learning communities (PLCs), a growing practice in the 21st century. Westside is one of very few high schools in the United States that have such a schedule, which resembles a college schedule in that it gives students class time and open time, so that no two days of a student's schedule are alike.

The modular schedule "creates opportunities during the day when both students and teachers are open for the one-on-one and small-group tutoring that often make the difference in learning. Each content area has a centralized area called an IMC [Instructional Materials Center] where students can go to get help from their teachers during their open times," says Natural Science teacher Michael Fryda.

The schedule also gives PLC teams the opportunity to meet on a weekly basis to collaborate on curriculum, instruction, and assessment. For example, Fryda, whose specialty is biology, meets with the two other Natural Science teachers, one of whom specializes in chemistry and the other in Natural Science. Each team member takes the lead in his or her designated content areas or special interests (Fryda has a special interest in astronomy), but they also plan activities as a team.

Fryda's PLC team also chose to study the relationship between students' test answers and the quality of their learning and found that multiple-choice questions, when well written and thoughtfully used, are an efficient way to assess knowledge of science content. The team also devised an evaluation method that avoids the "either-they-know-it-or-they-don't" approach by giving students credit for what they know.

This assessment strategy simply has students reflect on their answers to multiple-choice questions. For example, students can write "sure" or "unsure" next to each answer on a test to indicate their certainty. If they choose "unsure," they can receive partial credit by circling two answers they definitely know are wrong. After the tests have been graded, students can go back to the questions they missed and write an explanation of the correct answer, also analyzing why they chose an incorrect answer.

"This method makes students responsible for what they have learned and gives them a rare opportunity for self-evaluation," says Fryda. Students who self-correct also receive some credit back "so their grade more accurately shows this extra reflective learning experience," he adds. "Some teachers might view such planning and teaching as a threat to their individuality or academic freedom; we see it as 'the power of many' and our best chance to help all our students find success."

Because Fryda and his fellow PLC team members share an office, they frequently discuss how one another's lessons are progressing. "We give each other tips for instruction and let each other know what helped students learn and what didn't. The end result is that we all grow on a daily and sometimes hourly basis from immediate reflective feedback," Fryda says.

## Summertime Professional Development, from the Museum to the Field

Summer vacation is an excellent time for teachers to take advantage of professional development opportunities that involve learning from and working with scientists in the field or at museums. The Smithsonian Science Education Academies for Teachers, for example, open up access to the vast resources of the Smithsonian Institution to educators who come to Washington, D.C. These weeklong sessions focus on such topics as energy and motion and biodiversity and are tailored to the Science and Technology Concepts for Middle Schools curriculum developed by the National Science Resources Center (NSRC), a joint venture between the Smithsonian and the National Academies of Science. Through its Leadership Assistance for Science Education Reform (LASER) Center, the NSRC helps school districts reform their science programs using research-based best practices.

During the academies, teachers attend hands-on sessions and take field trips to get "behind-the-collection" looks into the work of scientists and curators at various Smithsonian museums and research centers. For example, during the *Energy and Motion* Academy, science teachers work in small groups to conduct an open inquiry using toy hovercrafts. Imagining how they might work with their own 8th grade students, the teachers push the gliding disks across the floor, carefully measuring displacement with meter sticks and timing their vehicles with stopwatches. The low-friction disks, which skim along the floor on a bed of air created by toy fans within, give teachers firsthand evidence of Newton's first law of motion: that an object in motion will remain so at a constant speed and direction unless countered by an external unbalanced force. Teachers are reminded that successful space travel depends on this law during a visit to the NASA Goddard Space Flight Center in Greenbelt, Maryland, the facility that managed the complicated repair mission of the Hubble Space Telescope and led NASA's mission to study Earth's environment.

Teachers who take part in the *Biodiversity* Academy are exposed to the diversity of life from a variety of ecosystems, including ocean, estuary, woodland, and jungle. At the Smithsonian Environmental Research Center in Edgewater, Maryland, teachers learn how to estimate the number of *Akashiwo sanguinea* (the microbes behind the oxygen-depriving red tide in the Chesapeake Bay) in one milliliter of water on a microscope slide. One day later and 75 miles inland, the same teachers work with scientists in the field to learn how to develop protocols to measure biodiversity in a woodland, using a meter stick, a measuring tape, data collection techniques, and a keen sense of observation.

Janice Russo, a Smithsonian academy participant who teaches a multigrade (6th–8th grade) science class, says that taking part in the training helped her focus on using inquiry in her classes. Russo teaches at Kazoo School in Kalamazoo, Michigan, which has adopted the University of Chicago's progressive education model incorporating cooperative learning, environmental education, and community involvement. Russo encourages her students to observe and record the details of what they take in with all their senses, to give them opportunities for using their inductive and deductive reasoning skills.

"I think because my classes last year involved dissection labs and a great deal of setup, I tended to rush the students so that I could make a specific point and then have time to clean up," Russo recalls. "The approach of the academy allowed us to take our time, to explore, to analyze, and to write. So I have slowed down this year. I'm allowing time for more reflection with each activity or lab."

In keeping with her fall semester theme of forces of flight, Russo also borrowed "the physics and toying-around lab" from the professional development experience. Her students examined friction, transfer of energy, and Newton's laws of motion by using such toys as a car with a magnet and a raceway with a magnetic strip, a Newton's Cradle, and a device that spins a disk into the air by means of a rip cord. "They loved it!" notes a satisfied Russo. Her students recorded their reflections on the lab in their science journals, including a drawing of the toy and their conclusions from small-group discussions about the role of energy in a toy's movement and integrating such new terms as *acceleration, magnetic energy, kinetic energy,* and *Newton's law of action and reaction.* "The students were fascinated with the transference of energy from one sphere to the other in the Newton's Cradle—and decided they would all like to make one," says Russo, who hunted for a design that would enable them to build their own.

By working as a teacher advocate at the Air Zoo, a local museum in Kalamazoo, Russo has also continued her museum learning experience. Thanks to her affiliation with the museum, students have access to its facilities, learning about the mechanics of flying from pilots and even taking an overnight field trip to study the airplanes at the museum. Russo also shares the wealth from her professional development with other teachers by participating in school workshops on Newton's laws and writing online lesson plans for the Air Zoo Skyspace E-cademy.

Opening each lesson with an inquiry lab grabs students' interest right away. "Students are more committed to understanding and enjoying the material if their interest is piqued," observes Russo. "I must admit that I didn't always approach my classes in this manner."

When it comes to adopting new ideas, science teachers are not much different from the students they teach. Stimulating professional development not only helps educators grasp the mysteries of the natural world more deeply through inquiry-based practices, but also shows them how to apply the new research about learning to good effect within a well-honed science curriculum.

## Reflections    ◆    ◆    ◆

Professional development for science teachers can go beyond traditional inservices and journal readings. Teachers can learn from mentors, in collegial learning communities, with the help of working scientists, or by pursuing further degrees. Giving science teachers the advice, support, and information they need to grow in their field opens a window onto their own practice and gives them the freedom to change, refine, or affirm what they do in the classroom. As teachers deepen their understanding of science content and of the special role of scientific inquiry, the insight they gain can help them to better engage students and revitalize their practice.

# References

Allen, R. (2001, Fall). Technology and learning: How can schools map routes to technology's promised land? *Curriculum Update*, 2–3.

Banilower, E. R., Boyd, S. E., Pasley, J. D., & Weiss, I. R. (2006, February). *Lessons from a decade of mathematics and science reform* (Prepublication copy). Arlington, VA: National Science Foundation. Retrieved March 29, 2006, from www.pdmathsci.net/reports/capstone.pdf

Barnard, J. D. (1962, January). Developments in science education. *Educational Leadership, 19*(4), 215–219.

Black, P., Harrison, C., Lee, C., Marshall, B., & Wiliam, D. (2003, April 22). *The nature and value of formative assessment for learning.* Paper presented at the annual meeting of the American Educational Research Association, Chicago. Retrieved June 7, 2007, from www.kcl.ac.uk/content/1/c4/73/57/formative.pdf

Black, P., Harrison, C., Lee, C., Marshall, B., & Wiliam, D. (2004). Working inside the black box: Assessment for learning in the classroom. *Phi Delta Kappan, 86*(1), 9–21.

Black, P., & Wiliam, D. (1998a). Assessment and classroom learning. *Assessment in Education, 5*(1), 7–71.

Black, P., & Wiliam, D. (1998b). Inside the black box: Raising standards through classroom assessment. *Phi Delta Kappan, 80*(2). Retrieved April 21, 2006, from www.pdkintl.org/kappan/kbla9810.htm

Black, P., & Wiliam, D. (2004). *International approaches to science assessment.* Paper commissioned by the Committee on Test Design for K–12 Science Achievement, Center for Education, National Research Council. Washington, DC: National Academy of Sciences. Retrieved June 20, 2006, from www7.nationalacademies.org/bota/International%20Perspectives.pdf

Brown, J. (2004). *Making the most of understanding by design.* Alexandria, VA: Association for Supervision and Curriculum Development.

Bybee, R. (2006, August). *Enhancing science teaching and student learning: A BSCS perspective*. Paper presented at the 2006 ACER Research Conference, Canberra, Australia.

Cavanaugh, S. (2006, November 15). Simple science difficult for urban students to grasp, NAEP study finds. *Education Week*, Web-only article. Retrieved Nov. 22, 2006, from www.educationweek.org

Committee on Science, Engineering, and Public Policy. (2007). *Rising above the gathering storm: Energizing and employing America for a brighter economic future*. Washington, DC: National Academies Press. Retrieved May 23, 2007, from www.nap.edu/catalog.php?record_id=11463#toc

DeBoer, G. (1991). *A history of ideas in science education: Implications for practice*. New York: Teachers College Press.

Donovan, S., & Bransford, J. B. (Eds.). (2005). *How students learn: Science in the classroom*. Washington, DC: National Academies Press.

Echevarria, J., & Colburn, A. (2006). Designing lessons: Inquiry approach to science using the SIOP model. In A. Fathman & D. Crowther (Eds.), *Science for English language learners* (pp. 99–101). Arlington, VA: National Science Teachers Association.

Echevarria, J., Short, D., & Powers, K. (2003). *School reform and standards-based education: How do teachers help English language learners?* Santa Cruz, CA: Center for Research on Education, Diversity & Excellence.

Elder, L., & Paul, R. (1996). *Universal intellectual standards*. Dillon Beach, CA: Foundation for Critical Thinking. Available: www.criticalthinking.org/resources/articles/universal-intellectual-standards.shtml

Grigg, W. S., Lauko, M. A., & Brockway, D. M. (2006). *The nation's report card: Science 2005* (NCES 2006–466). Washington, DC: U.S. Department of Education, National Center for Education Statistics. Retrieved June 7, 2007, from http://nces.ed.gov/nationsreportcard/pubs/main2005/2006466.asp

Harvard-Smithsonian Center for Astrophysics (Producer). (1987). *A private universe* [Videotape]. Cambridge, MA: Author.

Indiana Department of Education. (2006). *Indiana's academic standards, earth & space science I*. Indianapolis: Author. Retrieved May 24, 2007, from www.doe.state.in.us/standards/docs-Science/2006-Science-EarthSpace.pdf

Johnson, J., Arumi, A. M., Ott, A., & Remaley, M. H. (2006). *Reality Check 2006: Are American parents and students ready for more math and science?* New York: Public Agenda. Retrieved December 29, 2006, from www.publicagenda.org/research/pdfs/rc0601.pdf

Jorgenson, O., Cleveland, J., & Vanosdall, R. (2004). *Doing good science in middle school: A practical guide to inquiry-based instruction*. Arlington, VA: National Science Teachers Association.

Kelly, J., & Ponder, G. (1997). Evolution, chaos, or perpetual motion? A retrospective trend analysis of secondary science curriculum advocacy, 1955–1994. *Journal of Curriculum and Supervision, 12*(3), 228–245.

Lee, O., & Luykx, A. (2006). *Science education and student diversity: Synthesis and research agenda.* New York: Cambridge University Press.

Lutkus, A. D., Lauko, M., & Brockway, D. (2006). *The nation's report card: Trial Urban District Assessment Science 2005* (NCES 2007-453). Washington, DC: U.S. Department of Education, National Center for Education Statistics. Retrieved January 5, 2007, from http://nces.ed.gov/nationsreportcard/pubs/dst2005/2007453.asp#pdflist

Maatta, D., Dobb, F., & Ostlund, K. (2006). Strategies for teaching science to English learners. In A. K. Fathman & D. T. Crowther (Eds.), *Science for English language learners: K–12 classroom strategies.* Arlington, VA: National Science Teachers Association.

National Center for Education Statistics. (2006). *The condition of education 2006* (NCES 2006-071). Washington, DC: Author.

National Education Association. (1893). *Report of the Committee on Secondary School Studies.* Washington, DC: Government Printing Office. Retrieved January 12, 2007, from http://tmh.floonet.net/books/commoften/mainrpt.html

National Research Council. (1996). *National science education standards.* Washington, DC: National Academies Press. Retrieved January 4, 2007, from http://newton.nap.edu/html/nses

National Science Foundation. (1981, February). How the U.S. compares with other countries. *Educational Leadership, 38*(7), 368–370.

Perkins-Gough, D. (2006/2007, December/January). Special report: The status of the science lab. *Educational Leadership, 64*(4), 93–94.

Reiff, R. (2005). *Scientists' conceptions of scientific processes: Is the scientific method a one size fits all model?* Paper presented at the National Association for Research in Science Teaching (NARST), Dallas, Texas.

Reiff, R., Harwood, W., & Phillipson, T. (2002, January 10–13). A scientific method based upon research scientists' conceptions of scientific inquiry. In *Proceedings of the Annual International Conference of the Association for the Education of Teachers in Science, Charlotte, North Carolina.* Retrieved January 4, 2007, from http://edres.org/eric/ED465618.htm

Seiler, G. (2001). Reversing the "standard" direction: Science emerging from the lives of African American students. *Journal of Research in Science Teaching, 38*(9), 1000–1014.

Seiler, G. (2002). *Understanding social reproduction: The recursive nature of structure and agency within a science class.* Unpublished doctoral dissertation, University of Pennsylvania, Philadelphia.

Short, D., & Echevarria, J. (2004/2005, December/January). Teacher skills to support English language learners. *Educational Leadership, 62*(4), 8–13.

Singer, S. R., Hilton, M. L., & Schweingruber, H. A. (Eds.). (2005). *America's lab report: Investigations in high school science.* Washington, DC: National Academies Press.

Smith, C., Wiser, M., Anderson, C. W., Krajcik, J., & Coppola, B. (2004). *Implications of research on children's learning for assessment: Matter and atomic molecular theory.* Paper commissioned by the Committee on Test Design for K–12 Science Achievement, Center for Education, National Research Council. Washington, DC: National Academy of Sciences. Retrieved April 3, 2006, from www7.nationalacademies.org/bota/Big%20Idea%20Team_%20AMT.pdf

Thomas B. Fordham Institute. (2005, December 7). *Most K–12 state science standards don't make the grade.* Press release. Retrieved June 6, 2007, from www.edexcellence.net/foundation/about/press_release.cfm?id=20

Thompson, S. (2003, January 30). *Development of a framework to measure science teachers' inquiry perceptions and practices.* Paper presented at the annual conference of the Association for the Education of Teachers of Science, St. Louis, Missouri.

Tobin, K., Elmesky, R., & Seiler, G. (2005). *Improving urban science education: New roles for teachers, students, and researchers.* Lanham, MD: Rowman & Littlefield.

Wiggins, G., & McTighe, J. (2005). *Understanding by design.* Alexandria, VA: Association for Supervision and Curriculum Development.

Wilson, M. R., & Bertenthal, M. W. (Eds.). (2005). *Systems for state science assessment.* Washington, DC: National Academies Press. Retrieved March 31, 2006, from www.nap.edu/catalog/11312.html#toc

Yager, R. (Ed.). (2005). *Exemplary science in grades 9–12: Standards-based success stories.* Arlington, VA: National Science Teachers Association.

Yager, R. (2006, October 21). Science education can be science. In *Proceedings of symposium: Out-of-school science activities and science education* (pp. 41–62). Seoul: Korean Federation of Science Education Societies.

# Index

Page numbers followed by a *t* or *b* indicate tables or boxed material

# Related ASCD Resources: Science

At the time of publication, the following ASCD resources were available (ASCD stock numbers appear in parentheses). For up-to-date information about ASCD resources, go to www.ascd.org.

## Audio
*Math and Science Revolution: New Teaching Methods That Work* by Tracy Severns (#202154)
*Reading Strategies for the Science Classroom* by Mary Lee Barton (#505104)

## Networks
Visit the ASCD Web site (www.ascd.org) and click on About ASCD. Click on Networks for information about professional educators who have formed groups around topics like "Problem-Based Learning" and "Service Learning/Experiential Learning." Look in the "Network Directory" for current facilitators' addresses and phone numbers.

## Print Products
*Educational Leadership*, December 2006: Science in the Spotlight (#107029)
*Educational Leadership*, February 2004: Improving Achievement in Math and Science (#104027)
*Education Update*, April 2007: Making Science Matter (#107063)
*Priorities in Practice: The Essentials of Science, Grades K–6* by Rick Allen (#106206)
*Science: A Curriculum Handbook Chapter* by Jan Tuomi and Anne Tweed (#105014)
*Teaching Reading in Science (A Supplement to Teaching Reading in the Content Areas)* by Mary Lee Barton and Deborah L. Jordan (#302269)

## Video and DVD
*The Lesson Collection Tape 10 Physical Science: Visual Tools (Middle School)* (#400062)
*The Lesson Collection Tape 42 Science (Observation) (Middle School)* (#404459)
*The Lesson Collection Tape 45 Lab Prep (Acids and Bases) (High School)* (#404462)

For more information, visit us on the World Wide Web (http://www.ascd.org); send an e-mail message to member@ascd.org; call the ASCD Service Center (1-800-933-ASCD or 703-578-9600, then press 2); send a fax to 703-575-5400; or write to Information Services, ASCD, 1703 N. Beauregard St., Alexandria, VA 22311-1714 USA.